Eye of the Storm
Vairotsana's Five Original Transmissions

Radical Dzogchen

Eye of the Storm
Vairotsana's Five Original Transmissions

Foreword by Bhakha Tulku Pema Rigdzin

Translation and Commentary
Keith Dowman

Vajra Publications
Kathmandu, Nepal

Vajra Publications
Kathmandu, Nepal

Distribution:
Vajra Book Shop
PO Box 21779
Kathmandu
Nepal
http://www.vajrabooks.com.np
Tel/fax: 977-1-4220562

© 2006 by Keith Dowman. All rights reserved. No part of this book may be reproduced in any form or by any means, electronic or mechanical, including photography, recording, or by any information storage or retrieval system or technologies now known or later developed without permission in writing from the publisher.

ISBN 99946-644-8-4

Cover design by Nicholas Liber

Printed in Nepal

Dedicated to the anonymous masters of the great perfection, whoever they are, wherever they may be, however they appear.

Other Titles by Keith Dowman

Old Man Basking in the Sun
The Flight of the Garuda
The Sacred Life of Tibet
Power-places of Kathmandu
Boudhanath: The Great Stupa
Masters of Enchantment
The Power-places of Central Tibet: The Pilgrims Guide
Masters of Mahamudra
Sky Dancer: The Secret Life and Songs of the Lady Yeshe Tsogyel
The Nyingma Icons
The Divine Madman: The Life and Songs of Drukpa Kunley
The Legend of the Great Stupa
Calm and Clear: A Manual of Buddhist Meditation

Additional material relating to the *Eye of the Storm* can be found at www.keithdowman.net/dzogchen/eyeofthestorm.htm

Contents

Foreword by Bhakha Tulku — ix
Translator's Introduction — xi

The Cuckoo's Song of Gnosis — 1
Radical Creativity — 3
The Great Garuda in Flight — 9
Pure Golden Ore — 27
The Eternal Victory Banner — 35

Endnotes — 85

Appendices
I. The Tibetan Text and Sources — 91
II. Mind Series Jargon — 94

Bibliography — 107

Foreword by Bhakha Tulku Pema Rigdzin

The five texts translated into English in this book are considered the first transmission of Dzogchen Ati to Tibet. They were transmitted by a Tibetan monk called Vairotsana who distinguished himself not only in the field of translation, emerging as the greatest of the Tibetan lotsawas, but also as a traveler and pilgrim who left the Land of the Snows for the hills of the Hindu Kush to bring back a canon of Dzogchen texts from its closely guarded source. Returning from Oddiyana, where he had received the transmission of Dzogchen Ati from Shri Singha, he immediately translated these five tantras into Tibetan, and they became known as the Five Early Translations (*Nga-gyur-nga*). They constitute the root and essence of Dzogchen in Tibet—basic, raw Dzogchen precepts that are appropriately designated 'radical Dzogchen'.

Tulkus in the Nyingma tradition, considered emanations of the heart of reality, have been trained in the rites and devotions of the lineage, in the meditations and yogas of the vajrayana, in the Buddhist philosophy of India and Tibet and in the skillful means of assisting others not only on the path of liberation but in the amelioration of their suffering in samsara. But what precedes all of that in significance and priority, what gives it meaning and what facilitates the sharing of the buddha-dharma is Dzogchen Ati. This is the special, extraordinary teaching of our Nyingma lineage. The great masters, including Vairotsana, Padma Sambhava, and Vimalamitra, have all attained realization through Dzogchen, contemporary masters all owe their status to Dzogchen, and any attainment in the future will be based on the precepts of Dzogchen Ati.

Foreword

There is a vast number of texts revealing the various precepts of Dzogchen in the Mind, Matrix and Secret Precept Series, the Elaborate, Simplified, Simple and Ultra-simple Cycles, the Crown Pith and Ultra Pith teaching; but these five transmissions of Vairotsana, the core of the Mind Series, constitute the seed, root and branch of Dzogchen. Please remember that the greatest of the Five Early Translations, *The Vast Space of Vajrasattva*, was recited extempore by Garab Dorje, the first guru of the Dzogchen lineage, in his infancy. If the meaning of the verses is not clear to us, the commentary found in *The Ten Sutras* may provide illumination and the stimulus and inspiration that induce the realization of the great natural perfection, and beyond that there is nothing.

If the Tibetan dharma is to thrive in the West, it will be through the transmission of Dzogchen Ati, the apex path, the culmination of vajrayana Buddhism. Throughout history Dzogchen has been the subject of dispute amongst the various schools of philosophy in Tibet, but it is acclaimed by all yogins on the actual path of praxis. It is well known that it is the personal secret practice of H.H. The Dalai Lama himself. In its transmission to the western world the methods of conveyance may undergo certain changes, but the essence of Dzogchen will remain unchanging. This was the teaching of our lamas Dudjom Rimpoche and Kanjur Rimpoche in their Dzogchen mandala in Darjeeling in India where I first encountered Keith Dowman, the eminent translator of these texts.

I hope many people will read these texts and realize the heart meaning and spontaneously attain the realization of Dzogchen Ati and join those who have realized this ultimate truth but remain anonymous. May all sentient beings be free from samsara!

Bhakha Tulku Pema Rigdzin
Vairotsana Foundation
Los Angeles, California
www.vairotsana.org
Losar of the fire-dog year, 2006

Translator's Introduction

The nature of Dzogchen, or the Great Perfection, is perhaps best understood as the essence of all nondual mystical aspiration. Within the Tibetan context it lies at the heart of shamanism, Bon and Buddhism. Taking its cultural and linguistic references from Bon and Buddhism it may appear to be limited to those traditions; but to see its existential reality restricted to that cultural frame would contradict the Tibetan precepts that define it as utterly nonspecific and unconfined. Historically Buddhism provided the ground in which the precepts of the Great Perfection appeared, and certainly it still provides a rich and wonderful metaphysical field of reference. But the principles of radical Dzogchen are appropriate to every religious and cultural context. All religion and culture is transcended by its formless essence. It subsumes science and humanism today as it once incorporated shamanism and theism. It supersedes religion by shunning dogma and doctrine. It surpasses yoga and meditation by disavowing technique. It transcends the creativity of the human mind—whether as science or art—through identity with our intrinsic nature. Inclusivity defines the Great Perfection.

As mystical endeavor the quest for natural perfection may be conceived as long as human history. Surely it is hidden in the mysteries of Babylon and Egypt, Greece and Rome, in Indian Tantra, the Chinese Tao, Muslim Sufism, and in the Jewish Torah and the Christian heresies of the Albigensians, the Knights Templar and the Alchemists, if only because natural perfection is inherent in human being and cannot be suppressed. Deprived of a lineal tradition, guides and precepts, it may burst out spontaneously as an imperative of the human spirit, as it did in

Translator's Introduction

Europe and America in the 'sixties. Regardless of the cultural and religious context, the time and the place, the 'pathless path' of nondual illumination is always the same because the nature of the mind, being the origin of time and space, is one. It has happened, however, that in the twenty-first century the exemplars and custodians of this living tradition are the vajrayana Buddhists of the Tibetan plateau. Nondual mysticism finds its own ground everywhere in the scope of Tibetan Buddhism, particularly in the Kagyu mahamudra tradition, but it is in its earliest transmission into Tibet, when the tradition of the Ancients (Nyingmapa) was still in its incipient phase, that we find the most pure and unequivocal statement of the principles and poetic effusion of the meaning of the Great Perfection. That is what is termed radical Dzogchen.

Given that the oldest and earliest is not necessarily the best, nor any guarantee of quality—despite the beliefs of the creationists—the quality of pristine freshness nevertheless reverberates down the centuries from a culture on the verge of breakthrough. This quality may be discerned in eighth century Tibet and particularly in the work of the mystic and poet Vairotsana who at that time wrote down the five poems presented in this book. In his work there is a sense of the light of dawn spreading over the landscape to illuminate the darkness in one fell swoop. The word of Dzogchen had arrived to illuminate the murk of spiritualistic shamanism, to clarify the Buddhist options presented by India, China, Khotan, Brusha and Oddiyana and to exalt the lifestyles of the people of the Tibetan plateau. The freshness and vitality of Vairotsana's vision, written down when the Tibetan language was as young as English when Shakespeare wrote, still has the power to illuminate, although the shadows that are dispersed are cast by apocalyptic materialism and consumerism.

The power of Vairotsana's five original works may lie in the magic of 'transmission'—for that is how these poems are designated.

Translator's Introduction

Vairotsana did not attribute them to himself as the poet, but cast them in the mold of revelations of the human source of the Dzogchen tradition, Garab Dorje, the adiguru, in the land of Oddiyana, because all tantras, transmissions and precepts of Dzogchen are said to have the same timeless origin. The verses of each of the five transmissions, consisting generally of a quatrain of two slokas, can stand apart as didactic gems of Dzogchen expression, sometimes with only tangential connection between them, but they are better viewed as the facets of a crystal globe, each reflecting an aspect of the whole. The content of the transmissions is always the same—a unitary vision of the nature of mind. The nature of mind (where 'nature' can only mean 'essence') is pure mind, the one indivisible nondual mind of natural perfection. The holistic product may be personified as the all-good buddha Samantabhadra, who at the same time is the supreme source of the transmission and the transmission itself. The reader is identified, thereby, with the vision of each transmission.

The purpose of these five poems, then, is to induce a vision of natural perfection in the mind of the reader. This is not done by logic or causal connection but through the magic, the ambiguity, of poetry. As Patrul Rimpoche writes, 'We do not agree with the common dogma of traditionalists, that the only valid knowledge is mental knowledge tested by reason against textural and logical proof. Experiential understanding of the naked direct perception in primal awareness itself is the vision.'[1] In this sense, each of the five poems constitutes a direct introduction—if not initiation—into the nature of mind and the Great Perfection. The experience of the transmissions themselves is self-validating and any rational evaluation of their logic or terms of reference diminishes or blights them. The sole requisite for attaining the vision set down by the poet is a wide-open mind, and since all human beings are endowed with this mind the Great Perfection is available to everyone.

Translator's Introduction

The vision that these transmissions induce is not like a tantric mandala of buddhas or buddha-deities or patterned light-forms. There is not the slightest hint of symbolism, abstract or anthropomorphic. There is nothing to be seen that has any cultural specificity. There is no articulated abstruse metaphysical infrastructure to the vision. There is nothing that is not intrinsic to the nature of ordinary consciousness and the common light of day. In fact there is no trace of anything there at all. There is no structure to the vision whatsoever—the nature of the transmission is ultimately deconstructive. 'Simplicity' is the one single word that may describe it. It is a holistic vision in the sense that it is all-inclusive and nondual. It consists of direct naked perception of the nature of mind in every instant of experience.

The essence of the transmission is simple, direct perception. In the timeless moment of the here-and-now there is no space for projection and filtration and no time for evaluation, reflection and judgment. In this lies natural perfection. Herein lies the secret of nondual reality. When we speak of nondual mysticism, what is indicated is nothing but the clear light intrinsic to everyday perception; yet this perception and this function of awareness brings ultimate resolution to the human condition. All its dichotomies and contradictions are resolved in the unitary light of awareness in itself. If it can be said that conception and act exist, surely there is no gap between the initiation of the act and its fulfilment. The unitary moment is its own reward. Time and space are resolved in the all-inclusive wholeness of the moment. Embodiment is resolved in each moment. The paradox and antinomies of gender are resolved in the unity of the moment. This is transmission of the Great Perfection that does not impose a new, conditioned structure upon the mind, but reveals what is already, primordially present. It comes by way of confirmation, then, of what has always been known: that the nature of being, the nature of reality and the nature of mind are immanent as consummate perfection.

Translator's Introduction

There is nothing in this transmission that can be grasped or conceptualized or cultivated or practiced. To assimilate it into the logical intellect and spin it out as a philosophy or doctrine is to lose the point, just as the magic of poetry is lost in analysis. The transmission itself is a timeless event, like every moment of experience, arising as spontaneity, without cause or condition, so it cannot be developed into a yoga or a meditation practice. It cannot be turned into religion: there are no tenets of belief; neither devotion nor faith are conditions of its revelation; and no ritual interprets and structures it. It is simply an existential understanding of the here and now.

Vairotsana's five transmissions are compositions of deconstructive precept, expressing the Dzogchen vision of the nature of mind. Their primal impact upon a receptive reader may open a door into the vision of the Great Perfection. The rational mind, however, may concoct objections to such an unreferenced state and the attendant sense of identity loss. It is here that the commentary engages, providing elaboration through causal connection, lulling the intellect with its bromide, while undermining—deconstructing—the structure of the intellect by indicating the natural state of being, the supra-rational reality of Great Perfection that always lies immanent in the timeless moment. Here, the self-referential language of the tradition points at the unstructured ground of all language, and since this reality lies in an absence of any characteristics, attributes or functions the Upanishadic method of 'not this!' 'not that!' is employed. The mystery of the Great Perfection resides in its ineffable nondual reality that is a unity but at the same time a multiplicity. It is at once the source and the creation. It is inconceivable and inexpressible. It is enlightened mind or pure mind. To reveal all experience as this reality is the purpose of Dzogchen and the self-evident principles of the Dzogchen Mind Series are the transmission.

Translator's Introduction

There is nothing to do! 'Nonaction' or 'undirected action' defines the nature, ethos and dynamic of the Great Perfection. The here-and-now is a field of immanent sameness, and any attempt to affect it or change it by any technique is counter-productive. Any engagement of effort diminishes it. Seeking it inhibits its discovery. Nonaction is the precept that defines the natural inclination, or lack of any inclination, of the nature of mind in order that the manifest dynamic of the field of reality is uncrystallized in gnosis.

No meditation! No discipline! The pure mind that is the nature of all experience never comes into being or ceases to be; it cannot be created or destroyed: it has no structure. It cannot, therefore, be accessed through the structured activity of calculated discipline, and all goal-oriented meditation is such structured activity. Letting go of all practice whatsoever, including all the meditation techniques that condition the mind by focusing on an object of sight, sound or thought, there is no meditation and only an endless continuum of pure mind. Nonmeditation and no-structure is illustrated particularly in the fourth transmission, *Pure Golden Ore*.

No progress! No development in a graduated process! The moment is perfect and complete in itself and nothing superior can be effectuated. There is no possibility of attaining anything more desirable than the present moment. No personal growth is possible. Evolution towards a higher goal is precluded. There is no maturity to anticipate. The notion of process itself is redundant because it functions through time in a delusive linear pattern constructed by the intellect.

No place to go! The here-and-now is always complete in the present moment, so there is no path to follow, no quest, no journey to pursue and no destination. It is impossible to move towards or away from pure-mind reality, since it is always here and now. The inescapable universal and all-pervasive reality-process is ever-immanent. There is no destination other than the naturally liberating dynamic of the moment. This is taught particularly in *Radical Creativity*.

No discrimination! No prejudice or bias! The pristine awareness that is the mind's cognitive nature is utterly free of any judgmental inclination. It does not discriminate between what is good or bad, right or wrong. 'Good' and 'bad' are fictive labels projected upon a neutral screen, that in itself is incapable of bias. Whatsoever occurs in everyday experience, excluding nothing, is suffused by this primal awareness and moment by moment dissolves into it. All is perfect as it stands, so nothing is rejected or avoided and nothing is accepted or favored above anything else. Nothing is embraced or appropriated and nothing spurned or suppressed. All things are always all-good and activity is always undiscriminating. This is taught in the transmission of the first transmission, *The Cuckoo's Song*.

No-one and no-thing to change! The elements of experience, inner and outer, are part of a reality-field in which no indivisible particle can be isolated either in the laboratories of science or those of the mind. The natural unified field is a nondual reality. Every moment of experience is an ineffable expression of that field, and insofar as it is recognized as a field of cognitive being it is known as utterly perfect and complete in itself. It cannot be improved one iota. It cannot be changed or transformed into something other than pure awareness. Because our identity—nonidentity—lies in pure mind, whatever illusion of personality arises is utterly pristine.

No controller! No control! The control functions of the ego self-articulated in the rational mind are involuntarily superseded by the pristine awareness of the natural state of being. What appears to rise and fall as sequential instants of experience is insubstantial gossamer illusion and the dynamic of each perfect moment is spontaneity. Any belief in a substantial, material reality or of a 'self', a 'soul', an 'ens' or 'atman' is delusory. There is no controller on any level and so no control. The putative controlling intellect is superseded by the intrinsic dynamic of nonaction. The here-and-now is freeform display, perfect in its every permutation.

The consummation of these precepts and the transmissions themselves are predicated upon an intuitive realization of the nature of mind as intrinsically pure, an assumption that is authenticated, yet neither attested nor proven, in initiatory experience. 'Pure mind' is a rendering of the Buddhist word bodhichitta. In mahayana Buddhism the meaning of this word is suffused by the selfless compassionate ethic of the bodhisattva intent upon giving whatsoever is required to whomsoever is in need. More technically, it is translated as 'the thought of enlightenment'. In vajrayana Buddhism, where imminent buddhahood is assumed, it is translated as 'enlightened mind' or 'awakened mind'. In the Dzogchen Mind Series, this enlightened mind is the ground of all, all and everything, and the starting point, the process and the product in one. It subsumes the field of reality, the process of release, the nature of mind and primal awareness. Pure mind is the nondual natural state and so it cannot possess any definable quality, but in its vastness and depth, in its ineffable greatness, it exalts our natural state. Its primary endowment lies in direct and immediate enlightenment.

Pure mind is personified as Samantabhadra, the all-good primordial buddha—not a buddha to worship, but the actuality of every moment. Those he 'teaches', or manifests, are the buddhas and all the sentient beings upon the wheel of life, all free of transmigration and rebirth. His 'teaching', or manifestation, is the expression of our every moment of experience in a vision of reality as the matrix of all things and all things in themselves as one. The time of his teaching is the one clear timeless moment of

Translator's Introduction

past, present and future rolled into one. And the place of his teaching is the zero-dimensional reality-field.

In our state of natural perfection, the seemingly material world is consumed in its intrinsic nature as light by the pristine awareness inherent in every sensory perception. The four great elements—earth, water, fire and air—that are a condensation of their spatial essence constitute the reality-field itself, and the pure mind, wherein the delusive subjective and objective aspects of experience are unified, endows the reality-field with its own luminous display that never crystalizes as this or that. The subjective aspect of the unitary field, the sense of personal identity, is defined as the space where nothing can be found by seeking, nothing can be accomplished by endeavor, nothing whatsoever can be improved upon, and where there can be no progress or maturation. This is the natural state of primordial, pre-existent enlightenment. But because that state cannot become an object of focus, since it is in no way conceivable or imaginable, or determinable or demonstrable, it is better termed 'nonenlightenment'. Only in that sense is there universal enlightenment.

The expression of pure mind is the compassion that suffuses our experience like water in milk. Such compassion is the potential of every possible convention and variation of human character and personality, every quality and attribute, every affectation and every foible, every vice and virtue, and every weirdness and extreme manifestation of being on the wheel of life. The psychological diversity of experience therein is expressed in the equivocal terms of men, gods, titans, hungry ghosts, animals and devils. Yet the wheel of life is the expression of the compassion of pure mind and compassion is the wheel of life. The primordial buddha Samantabhadra embraces the totality of pure mind as its essential emptiness, its radiant luminosity and its compassionate expression.

Translator's Introduction

The vast spaciousness of pure mind is personified as Vajrasattva and primal awareness is his exaltation. The spaciousness of reality is spontaneously cognitive in a nondual process and Vajrasattva represents the individuation of that process. The process is inherently liberating so that there can never be any experience whatsoever that is not spontaneously and momentarily released. His ineluctable presence provides that assurance. Primal awareness of the field of reality is a constant and therefore Vajrasattva receives his name 'Immutable Being'. The vajra is a symbol of his immovable and imperturbable nature of constant luminous awareness. His immutable dynamic is the freedom of the Great Perfection.

Insofar as there is only pure mind in our experience, insofar as the vajra is inherent in every moment, there can never be either separation or non-separation from Vajrasattva, which is a manner of stating the ineffable immanence of the natural state of being in the great perfection. So there can never be any obstacle to that natural state. What appears to obstruct the recognition of intrinsic cognitive spaciousness is attachment to the mere shimmering of gossamer phantasm, which is like a film of tarnish on pure gold. If this attachment appears to veil the nature of mind, then what is required is a fortuitous lurch into an intuition of the attachment itself as pristine awareness—a flash of realization or a recollection of initiatory experience. If the problems that arise from the exigencies of personal karma intrude into the forefront of our minds and a sense of constant interruption of the natural flow obsesses us, then what fortuitously arises is intuition of the intrinsic clarity of the glitch itself. Thus the apparent obstacles that arise in the mind provide the key to their own resolution.

Some people are convinced that their desire, anger and emotional confusion are a thick veil over their enlightened mind, but the recognition of the light and pure pleasure in the marvelous display of energetic expression dissipates such delusive beliefs. Some are convinced that the implacable logic of the intellect and attachment to its pleasures create the trap that locks in the spaciousness, but intellectual constructs themselves and every train of thought constitute a door into Vajrasattva's vast space. To overcome what appear to be emotional and intellectual obstacles, people commit themselves to disciplines of lifestyle and morality, yoga and meditation, setting themselves the goal of freedom from attachment and rebirth, but the anxiety entailed by prostituting the moment for some future benefit and striving for a conceptual goal is resolved naturally in the relaxation of nonaction. The disease of calculated endeavor and goal orientation that is called spiritual materialism is healed by the spontaneous and ineluctable intuition of the pure nature of mind.

The futility of trying to catch what is already in the cage or to grope all around for spectacles that are already on the end of the nose inevitably dawns upon the goal-obsessed yogi or yogini and it is well that we are prepared by recollection of the spaciousness and radiance that we know from fortuitous initiation into the nature of mind. Decisively, we arrive at the place where the moral imperatives instilled by the plain logic and symmetry of belief in karmic concatenation are seen to provide still more of the same anxious transmigration from one neurotic trap to another and where relaxation into the timeless moment of the here-and-now—doing nothing—allows the clarity and emptiness of the natural state of being to shine through. When the compulsions of karmic causality and belief in moral imperatives fall away and dissolve and we surrender to the buddha-dynamic of spontaneous contemplation, pristine awareness naturally prevails, superseding any residual trust in the world of karma.

With recognition of the reality thus defined, there is simultaneous recognition of the samaya commitments of Dzogchen—absence, openness, spontaneity and unity. By their very nature, these samayas cannot be guarded or sustained. On the contrary, awareness of their actuality is a constant and natural presence that can never be vouchsafed or gainsaid. These samayas are not provisional commitments to be renounced upon reaching any goal. They are the reality of buddhahood here and now that can be expressed as one single commitment which is to pristine awareness itself. This awareness always has primacy. It is co-extensive and co-terminal with the space of equality which exalts all cognition as gnosis. Gnosis is the direct experience of the moment in which there is no subjective or objective component, although in it the delusive and the non-delusive are inextricably mixed. It is intrinsic awareness of being effervescing in the timeless wholeness of purity and impurity. It is the common light of day.

What constitutes the display of Samantabhadra may not differ in kind from the forms of the neurotic universes that are being neutralized. The retinue of Samantabhadra is composed of all buddhas and sentient beings, and the diaphanous radiance of rainbow light suffuses the very illusions that once seemed so concrete, tangible and cloying. The projections of the psychological environments of hungry ghosts or power-freaks, for example, may still be in place, but now the hair-raising figments of imagination that populate those environments are like the ferocious yet empty masks of lama-dance. Further, in the human realm, many people, particularly Buddhists, have entered the various graduated paths to enlightenment. Each rests on his own level which is complete and perfect in itself. All the activities of gods and men are complete and perfect in themselves and although they may pursue goal-oriented activity and constantly create or encounter seeming glitches in the universal process of awakened reality, the liberating capacity of Vajrasattva who suffuses the five elements that constitute embodiment in an apparent concrete environment is always immanent.

Translator's Introduction

The different lifestyles and the associated visions, therapies and meditation techniques, employed by monks and nuns, laymen and women, yogis and yoginis, and tulkus and dakinis may be conceived of hierarchically in a pyramid of increasingly destructured mind. This ninefold hierarchy is employed by the commentary on the root verses of the texts as an index of different mind states and allows a focus upon the varying progressive approaches that although delusive as paths to nondual reality are perfect in themselves. Nine is a perfect or infinite number in shamanic numerology, so that the nine conventional approaches or levels that provide the mainstay subsume all others. By the same token, the nine levels of meaning in the transmission, each directed towards and heard by those for whom it is relevant, subsume all other levels in the quest for the nature of mind. Further, as the traditional metaphor has it, just as a king never leaves his palace without his entourage in appropriate association, so Dzogchen Ati is always accompanied by a retinue composed of the innumerable disciplines that seek to modify or improve the human condition—for the mark of human birth is the impulsion to attain happiness. The teacher of the Great Perfection, Samantabhadra, incorporates a vast all-inclusive retinue of beings, each preoccupied by his personal path on which appropriate transmission may be fortuitously received.

The nine approaches or levels from the apex are atiyoga, anuyoga, mahayoga, tantra or sattva-yoga, ubhayayoga, kriyayoga, and the praxis of bodhisattvas, hermits and disciples. On the level of atiyoga the hyper-yogin is adept in the recognition of all experience as transmission of the great perfection. On the level of anuyoga identity of reality and gnosis, space and awareness is shown, so that every mind-created phenomenon becomes primal awareness. On the mahayoga level the elements of the psycho-organism and the elements of perception and the sense fields are revealed as our timeless enlightened identity; mahayoga is taught so that the structure of the conditioned mind is recognized as the five buddhas. In the mind-created vision of tantra-yoga, although the passions are not abandoned, attachment to them is utterly forsaken and sacred substances are literally enjoyed; thereby, in signless, open vulnerability, primal awareness is facilitated and the four consorts are recognized. In ubhaya-yoga the identity of clear light with its colored diffusion, between self-sprung awareness and the sensory phantasmagoria is taught. In the praxis of disciples engaged in listening and learning, hermits in ascetic retreat, and bodhisattvas in pursuit of loving kindness, the nature of mind involuntarily shines through.

Finally, to distinguish between the recipients of these transmissions, there are those who are ready vessels with an innate affinity for the natural great perfection. This type attains the vision merely by reading the transmission or by hearing the precepts—thus 'liberation by hearing'. Through recognition of the natural state of mind, whatever arises is released and dissolves immediately, leaving no trace. The Dzogchen yogin or yogini's existential modality is then commensurate with the imprint of a bird in the sky. All experience is like a dance and like the free-play of sensual pleasure. There is no meditation and no meditator. If glitches arise they are immediately turned into a timeless moment of mental effort and become a door back into the space of the great perfection that actually can never be relinquished. He or she assimilates the affirmation and confirmation of initiatory experience that atiyoga provides in the transmission and is absorbed without reflection in the nondiscriminatory totality of an anonymous body of light.

Then there are those who see the vision of Samantabhadra clearly through this transmission but lose it thereafter. Through a verbal introduction, or some initiatory experience, they accept the vision as the apotheosis of human nature and with subsequent intimation of the nature of mind they enjoy nonmeditation. But then immersed in the mundane concerns of life—profit and loss, love and hate, success and failure, fame and fortune—they see the figments of their minds as personality isolates interacting in a concrete environment, and becoming attached to seemingly external phenomena the vision of Samantabhadra is lost. Fortuitously and inevitably, however, the vision and nonmeditation does return to mind, like the rising sun, and with increased familiarity and intimacy allows fearless, wholehearted, surrender to the nature of mind. Pristine awareness then resumes its natural primacy. Confidence in nonaction is reaffirmed. Belief in mental constructs slackens. Fictive projections fade away. Through the temerity of recognition of the supreme source in whatever arises, in the bardo, natural perfection is recognized in a body of light.

Then there are those who perceive the vision as through a glass darkly, and overruled by judgmental thought while reading or hearing the transmission conceptualize it and analyze it and become susceptible to doubt. In a rationalistic process the vision is externalized and distanced and becomes a subtle and substantial goal to be achieved with a coincident sense of separation and inadequacy in the face of it. Samsara is divorced from nirvana in this process of linear thought through time and caught on the horns of conflicting emotion we are susceptible to expectation and apprehension. 'Our actions are determined by karma,' we say. 'We are subject to karmic retribution. We are bound to the inevitable cycle of transmigration on the wheel of time.' 'We have received Samantabhadra's transmission and it has given us a glimpse of perfection for a moment. But we are left with only an intellectual understanding and it has not affected our way of being.' 'We live in a world of preferences and partiality, attachments and aversions, discrimination and judgment, hopes and fears.' 'We are not ready,' we demur with a sense of inadequacy. 'We are just beginners. We need to improve ourselves, to be good and virtuous, to control our energy patterns, to set goals and attain them, to climb the ladder of spiritual purity.'

Riddled by such intellectual and emotional conflict, infected by hopes and fears, we conclude that something must be done, that remedial action is prescribed in order to attain the nondual state of the vision. Such readers may go on to devote their lives to a graduated path of endeavor, practicing some meditation technique or yoga, failing to adopt recognition of the perfection of their natural state.

On the other hand, many hear the transmission and think about it and lacking any initiatory experience they reject it and turn away. For them there never can be anything but the natural state of perfection, yet they live as beggars on the wheel of transmigration believing that the material world is concrete and the states of mind in which they find themselves are real. Attached to the pleasant and averse to the painful, unknowingly they await the revelation of the nature of mind. So it is said.

Vairotsana: The Great Translator

In the vision of the Great Perfection, the five transmissions are Dharmakaya Samantabhadra himself. Through the medium of Vajrasattva, and the uniting of vowels and consonants, the transmission arises as a timeless display of compassionate emanation in the nature of mind. This revelation is known as Vajra-Delight, or Garab Dorje, who is also the adiguru of the Dzogchen lineage. Vairotsana was his Tibetan translator.

In the eighth century, in Central Asia, the locus of political and cultural vigor still lay in Tibet. The nomads of a united Central Tibet had created a military empire that stretched from Persia to China, from Nepal to Mongolia. Their shamanic heritage, under the influence of the sophisticated cultures that were now part of their domain, was in the process of transformation. Those cultures in the main were Buddhist, though of various hues, and along with the cavalry and diplomats, the traders and artisans, traveling the

Translator's Introduction

Himalayan trade routes and all bound for Lhasa, were chan monks from China, vajrayana panditas from Bengal, mahayana scholars from Bihar and Khotan, tantric yogis from Kashmir and the Valley of Nepal, Hindu sadhus from South India and Bon shamans from the old kingdom of Zhangzhung that had dominated the Tibetan plateau before the rise of the Yarlung Valley dynasty. Buddhist temples of stone had been built in this land of yak-hair tents and although the majority of the conservative tribal nobility opposed it, the king sponsored a monastic academy directed by a Bengali abbot who had ordained a small band of Tibetan monks.

Less than a days' walk up the Yarlung Tsangpo river from the site of the new monastery, in one of the fertile side valleys to the north called Nyemo, was the village of Jekhar. It was from here that the young Vairotsana was called to Buddhist ordination by the Bengali abbot Shantarakshita. Being one of the brightest and most strongly motivated of the young monks, he was chosen to focus on the study of language. Existential concerns were a constant preoccupation amongst a significant element of the royal court, some of whom had also received Buddhist ordination along with Vairotsana, and discussion with visiting monks from abroad was fervent and often heated. A yogi-exorcist called Padma Sambhava who had been invited to Samye from Kathmandu had been successful in confronting the Bon shamans and Buddhists were in the ascendant. This itinerant exorcist, a Buddhist tantric sadhu wandering the Himalayan valleys for years, leaving a trail of disconsolate dakini-consorts behind him, had already gained notoriety in Tibet by seducing a local princess. He was originally from a kingdom in the far west of the Himalayas called Oddiyana, the land of the dakinis. Oddiyana had become associated with an extraordinary discipline called Dzogchen, known to the Yarlung Tibetans through their Bon confreres from Zhangzhung who had trans-Himalayan connections in Brusha and other kingdoms in the valleys of the upper Indus tributaries. Perhaps as a reaction to an overload of doctrinal dispute, perhaps based upon a natural inclination towards an effortless discipline promising immediate fulfillment, perhaps due to a secret word passed on by Padma Sambhava himself or by another itinerant yogi, a nexus of opinion formed at Samye that Dzogchen was the answer to the existential problems of the Tibetan people. Subsequently, under the auspices of King Trisong Detsen, Vairotsana and a friend were chosen to travel to Oddiyana to bring back to Tibet the Dzogchen transmission.

The direct route to Oddiyana lay up the Yarlung Tsangpo valley, passing Mount Kailash to the south, and then continuing through the ancient Zhangzhung heartland and down the Indus valley through Ladakh to Kashmir and Brusha and thence south to what is now Swat and eastern Afghanistan. Vairotsana's journey to Oddiyana and his meeting with the master Sri Singha, is the stuff of legend. Near the Dhanakosha Lake, in a sandalwood forest, he found the old master Shri Singha, originally from the Chinese side of the Taklamakan desert, living in a nine storied pagoda. He needed first to pass a protective yogini-crone, a doorkeeper who barred his way, but with a totally ingenuous mind and a stash of gold coins he passed her by and gained audience with the master. Shri Singha heard his plea for the extraordinary Dzogchen teaching and knew that it was destined that the transmission should pass to Tibet. Yet he kept Vairotsana waiting until the following morning. Then he promised the young Tibetan that he would grant him the transmission on the condition that he joined the panditas studying the gradual, causal approaches during the day and only at night time receive the atiyoga teaching. Due to the Oddiyana king's jealousy of Dzogchen Ati, its propagation had been proscribed, so during the nights of transmission the master wrote down the Mind Series transmissions on white silk with goat-milk ink which would become visible only when exposed to heat. Then at Vairotsana's further urging, Shri Singha granted him the Matrix Series precepts in the black, white and variegated modes. Still Vairotsana was not satisfied, but Shri Singha would give him no more.[2]

After this long and intense exposure to Shri Singha, Vairotsana was finally prepared to meet the adiguru of the Dzogchen tradition, the nirmanakaya emanation of Vajrasattva, Garab Dorje himself. This apocryphal encounter occurred in a cremation ground called Dumasthira, the place of fire and smoke, and Vairotsana emerged from the meeting with the transmission of the entire sixty-four hundred thousand Dzogchen verses and a body of light.

He returned to Central Tibet by means of his newly acquired speed-walking facility. Welcomed with all due honor, residing in the royal palace, he began a period of intense translation firstly of the five transmissions, which became known as the Five Early Translations. During this period he taught King Trisong Detsen the precepts that he was translating in the same way that Shri Singha had taught him—the progressive approach during the day and Dzogchen Ati at night. Proximity to the court, however, was to bring his honeymoon in the eye of the storm to an end and at the same time contrive to preserve his Dzogchen lineage in Tibet during its period of greatest vulnerability. One of the king's consorts had been influenced by the long and jealous arm of the King of Oddiyana, and in order to curtail Vairotsana's teaching activity she accused him of raping her and sought to have him banished. The king was reluctant to believe his queen, but eventually succumbing to her repeated denunciation he exiled Vairotsana to Tsawa Rong in the country of Gyelmo Rong in Kham, in eastern Tibet. There Vairotsana taught Dzogchen to three yogins, amongst whom Yudra Nyingpo was the principal, establishing a separate and enduring Dzogchen tradition in the east of the country.

TRANSLATOR'S INTRODUCTION

When the climate at court became more clement, Vairotsana was recalled from exile and continued to teach and translate in Central Tibet. The principal recipients of his transmission were Nyak Jnana Kumara and the Khotanese queen Liza Sherab Dronma. Later he was invited to Khotan and taught there and passed away in that foreign land. Vairotsana is the root of all the Tibetan Dzogchen lineages.[3]

Notes on the Text

The Five Early Translations are found in *The Collected Tantras of Vairotsana*, a compendium that was probably compiled in the twelfth century. During the same period they were assimilated to *The Supreme Source*, the encyclopedic Dzogchen Mind Series tantra, which took pride of place as the first text in the atiyoga section of *The Collected Tantras of the Ancients*. This last collection went through various mutations and is our primary source of Dzogchen texts today (see Appendix I). The second text in the atiyoga section of *The Collected Tantras of the Ancients* is called *The Ten Sutras*, a commentary on Vairotsana's five transmissions and a rich source of Dzogchen precepts in itself. It is this text that has provided our commentary. It was written by an unknown author again probably in the twelfth century.

In the text herein the lines that introduce each of the transmissions are a synthesis of material taken from *The Supreme Source* and *The Ten Sutras*. The root verses are translations of the best readings we could elicit from the various sources. The commentary on the verses is a paraphrastic translation of *The Ten Sutras'* commentary with explanatory notes interpolated. *The Eternal Victory Banner: The Vast Space of Vajrasattva*, by far the longest of the transmissions, is divided into twenty-seven parts, or 'timeless moments', found in *The Collected Tantras of Vairotsana* edition. The headings to the commentaries to the *Victory Banner* verses are taken from *The Ten Sutras*. The final line of the

xxx

commentary is a summation of the meaning of the entire verse. The annotation to the text indicates only a few of the discrepancies between the various sources.

Acknowledgments

With deep gratitude and deference I thank all the masters of the Tibetan tradition for their transmission, in particular Dudjom Rimpoche and Kanjur Rimpoche, who were both heart-sons of the great treasure-finder Trinle Jampa Jungne; also to my friend and mentor Bhakha Tulku Pema Rigdzin, a Dzogchen yogi, for all his kindness; to Chogyal Namkhai Norbu, the terton-king of our age, for his spacious understanding; to Adriano Clemente for his spadework on the texts; and to Terese Coe and Sondra Hausner for their immaculate professional and sensitive editing.

Keith Dowman
at the Great Stupa of Boudhanath
in the Kingdom of Nepal
in the wood-bird year, 2005.

The Cuckoo's Song of Gnosis

In Tibet's ancient shamanic tradition, the cuckoo was a magical bird, the king of birds. As the cuckoo's first call is the harbinger of spring, so the six lines of the *Cuckoo's Song of Gnosis* introduce gnostic reality. In this seminal transmission, Samantabhadra defines himself as spontaneously complete and perfect nonaction. It incorporates the precept of undiscriminating joyous activity. This is the root text of the Dzogchen Mind Series.[4]

Hey, Mahasattva, Magnificent being, listen!

The nature of multiplicity is nondual
and things in themselves are pure and simple;
being here and now is construct-free
and it shines out in all forms, always all good;
it is already perfect, so exertion is redundant
and spontaneity is ever-immanent.

All experience, the entire phantasmagoria of the six senses, the diverse multiplicity of existence, in reality is without duality. Even if we examine the parts of the pure essence of mind in the laboratory of the mind, such specifics are seen to be illusive and indeterminate. There is nothing to grasp and there is no way to express it. The suchness of things, their actuality, left just as it is, is beyond thought and inconceivable and that is the here-and-now. Yet diversity is manifestly apparent and that is the undiscriminating, all-inclusive sphere of the all-good buddha, Samantabhadra. Total perfection has always been a fact and there has never been anything to do to actuate this immaculate completion. All endeavor is redundant. What remains is spontaneity and that is always present as our natural condition.

If the six lines are divided into three pairs of verses describing Dzogchen vision, meditation and action respectively, the first two lines express the view that pure mind is an ineffable singularity and cannot be analyzed; the second two lines indicate nonmeditation as the natural state of Samantabhadra's display; and the third couplet shows action as the non-directed action—nonaction—of spontaneous awareness.

Radical Creativity

Samantabhadra's radical creativity is the miracle of illusory display emanated in every moment. It lies in the freeform field of reality that is the dynamic of nonaction. In a more limited sense, however, radical creativity is evident here in the soft touch of Samantabhadra's breath of inspiration that informs these pith instructions. This is a transmission that embodies specific instruction. It teaches that there is no path to traverse and no distinction to be made in pure mind reality.[5]

Hey, Mahasattva, Magnificent Being, listen!

1

All and everything emanates from me,
so all and everything, whatever appears,
is revealed as transmission,
revelation of the timelessly pure reality-field.

The path is the process of Samantabhadra's entire emanation in a timeless moment. In this respect every moment is identical and complete in itself and there can be no progress or development in or of pure mind. There can be no gradual increase or decrease of realization through time. Further, if all is one in the moment, how can there be any valid differentiation of pure mind from reality or, indeed, any distinctions whatsoever? Samantabhadra's all-inclusive momentary emanation is the nonreferential field of reality, which is his transmission and his instruction. The here-

and-now is pure mind, the field of reality and Samantabhadra's complete transmission. There is nothing else.

2

*All outer and inner is the timeless field of reality
and in such an immaculate field of play
buddha and sentient beings are not distinct—
so why try to change anything?*

Pure mind and reality are one in the reality-field and it is quite impossible to make any distinction. We say that all phenomena, whatever exists, composed of earth, water, fire, air and space, is external, and that pure mind and the nature of reality are internal. But this is idle speculative thought imputing mere nominal meaning where there is no real basis for it. The field of reality is an all-inclusive unity. In this timeless sphere of activity there is no distinction between buddha and sentient beings. It is impossible to improve on the timeless moment—it is already perfect and complete, the all-good Samantabhadra. It cannot be altered or transformed because it is the immutable Vajrasattva.

3

*There is no ambition in effortless, fully potentiated creativity
and such freeform spontaneous perfection is always the same;
in the pure field of reality, where the conception and the act are one,
however misguided how can we innocents do any wrong?*

A moment of bodhi-reality is primordially perfect and lacks any goal-orientation or ulterior intent; it has no desire. It is free of all aspiration. It is uncontrolled and uncontrollable freeform display. It is always the same in the ultimate equality of pure mind. The meaning is always the same. Since it is complete and perfect as it stands, there is nothing at all to do, and there never was anything to do, and thus activity is freeform display. All strenuous practice is rendered effete. Here, both impulse and its simultaneous actualization and both immaculate subject and object are the pure field of reality. In this milieu it is impossible to err, regardless of our naive beliefs and intractable habits. Nothing we fools can do can defile this pure space.

4

The pure-pleasure union of sentient behavior,
conceived by the deluded as a perverse path,
is identical to the pure process of Samantabhadra:
whoever understands such equality is buddha, lord of all.

Pure-pleasure union, sensory or sexual, as an integral part of human conduct, or as a tantric path, is reviled as immoral or perverse by the ignorant. But the course of human behavior, from the beginning, is inseparable from Samantabhadra's transmission as revealed above—freeform play. These two paths are actually one. The lord of past, present and future buddha is he who realizes these apparently incompatible modes as identical.

All dualities, all dualistic structures, are spontaneously resolved in the absolute equality of Dzogchen. This includes the duality of the delusive path of gender union and the pure mind modality where the vision and the act are one. The apparent duality of the gender principles of skillful means and insight united in pure pleasure is actually always a unity from the beginning, a primordial unity, pulled apart (in anuyoga) only in order to recognize it as a unity and always for the first time.

5

On the delusive, extremist path, thinking, 'I' and 'Mine',
deluded innocents enter a structured path of dharma practice

with no chance to realize that it leads nowhere:
how can reality ever be found by seeking?

The teacher who talks in terms of 'I' and 'Mine' implies the existence of a substantial self—or soul—in an individual who must strive to gain and hold something that he lacks. This conventional way of thinking is called 'extremist' because of its lack of a sense of middle way where the 'I' is deconstructed and the notion of possession becomes a fallacy. Such a teacher draws his students into a conceptual, progressive, goal-oriented dharma practice, where there is a presumption that the graduated path has an attainable goal and that realization can be obtained through analysis and where there is no possibility of spontaneous realization. The path of ritual performance and religious practice has no end. In the Great Perfection there is no path—only the timeless modality of momentary unfoldment. Thus the nature of reality cannot be found by seeking; it is already present. The mind cannot objectify its own nature, so reality cannot be found by searching for it. Seeking it would be like a dog chasing its own tail.

6

The instruction of monkey-like masters who lack direct insight
is fraught with false concepts of preparation and technique;
so the master who cleans the tarnish from pure gold,
the authentic teacher, the most precious resource,
he is worth the ransom at any price.

A monkey mimics without understanding, like a teacher who gives precept and transmission without the valid basis of understanding that is direct insight into the nature of mind. Such teaching induces a conceptual notion of the path, a specific starting point and a goal in the mind of the disciple, involving preparation, supports and technique. The master who sees the nature of mind has eradicated any implication of a conditioned path. This is likened to removing any fine film of tarnish from pure gold through the application of black alum—a traditional practice. No refinement, like separating the dross from pure gold, is necessary. The teacher's transmission of this pathless path is worth to his students whatever price must be paid. In early times the student proved his commitment by offering gold to the master.

The Great Garuda in Flight

The garuda is a giant mythical bird, like an eagle. In the mountains he glides high in the sky, wide wings outstretched, riding the currents of air, occasionally beating his wings in unison. He seems to put no effort into his flight. He is utterly alone there. He appears to be flying purely for the joy of it. He has mastery.

Samantabhadra, Pure Mind, taught this seminal transmission on effortless perfection, undirected freeform action, so that the mind can rest at ease. It shows that there is nothing substantial in the mind, that there is no quest to pursue and no possible progress on a path towards a goal, that reality cannot be demonstrated or proven in any way and that it is immune to inflating or deflating evaluating bias.

Within this uncompromising description of the great garuda in flight—the Dzogchen yogi in a nondual modality—there appear references to glitches and veils and also allusions to the keys to the doors through which existential miasma may be forsaken.[6]

Hey, magnificent immutable being, listen!

1

Hey! This freeform field, illusive like space,
nowhere located, has no object of focus;
an unstructured experiential process
it occurs in the slightest subtle projection:
the concept of pure being, indeterminable,
itself is self-sprung awareness,
an ubiquitous, unthinking, authentic presence,
and this illusive freeform field needs no alteration.

The field of nonaction, a freeform field of reality, is the dharmadhatu itself, and its pristine awareness is everywhere naturally present. The projected fields of dualistic perception are instantaneously transcended as a spontaneously emergent, nonobjective field of reality. Therein lies the process.

Pure being, the dharmakaya, conceived as an object in contrived meditation has no content, no specific qualities and no actuality and hence the ubiquitous self-sprung awareness. Think of pure being—a thoughtless, boundless space of equality—and the mind is filled by the nondual actuality of spontaneous pristine awareness. Pure mind is at once the sole cause and effect and for that reason, when relativistic thought-forms arise in pure being, they spontaneously emerge as a freeform field of pristine awareness.

The reality of nondual perception is an integrated field in which objects cannot be located or focused as discrete entities. The innate tendency of the intellect to concretize and reify is perceived here as a subtle projection or 'dedication' that is immediately recognized as the field of reality. It is as if the structuring, conceptualizing, tendency of conditioned mind instantaneously unfolds into an insubstantial, unstructured, inconceivable, field of reality. Thus the dualism of subjective knower and any objective factor never arises. There is only ever pure being, simultaneously a concept of emptiness and an existential reality. Any slight projection that gives intimation of a putative duality is immediately released by itself. Each thought and concept has intrinsic its own automatic release function: as pristine awareness it swallows itself.

Thus the natural field of reality cannot be improved upon and there is nothing at all to be done to attain it. Indeed, there is no object to address in this field, so how can anything be done to it? Any goal-oriented meditative technique employed to discover it is a vain counter-productive attempt that seeks to turn it into an object; but the nature of the causal method itself cannot but find the reality of the pure essence of mind.

2

Seeking the essence through derivative phenomena,
enjoy it only through its nonconceptual aspect:
the manifest essence is just pure being.

The field of experience is perfected as it stands and nothing needs to be done to actualize it as pure being. In whatever manner the pure essence of mind appears, the appearance itself finds its own intrinsic reality. Its seeming appearance is recognized as inconceivable and so its manifestation is free of mental structuring and only as such, free of constructs, can it be enjoyed. 'Derivative phenomena' is to be understood as the relative world that arises through the mutual dependence of twelve causes and conditions (ignorance, habitual tendencies, consciousness, name and form, six sensory fields, contact, feeling, craving, existence, birth, old age and death). But what appears to be interdependent phenomena is the freeform field of the pure essence of mind. 'The field of reality, unchangeably empty, is known through reflections in the nature of mind.'[7] The analysis of samsara as a twelve-fold causal chain may be employed in the meditation technique whereby the emptiness of each link is established and the source of samsara revealed. But in the view disclosed here the twelve concepts in themselves—nothing but pure being—are the means to their own immediate consummation (see also verses 24 and 25).

Relaxing into every concept with an empty mind, the pristine awareness of pure being, which is the individuated pure essence of mind, is spontaneously present. Thus the marvelous display of Samantabhadra is enjoyed as its inconceivable, unstructured nature. Since the pure essence of mind is intrinsic to all, nothing but pure being can ever arise out of it and there is nothing else to achieve. To put it another way, the natural expression of pure being is its own antidote and it is reflexively released into itself.

3

This one nucleus, indivisible, unpatterned,[8]
is the nonspecific actuality of pristine awareness;
in that vivid, unthought, wide-open essence,
on the path of purity lies sovereign equality.

This one indivisible nucleus that can never be particularized or localized is the pure mind essence evoked in the previous verse. Within it pristine awareness, being noncomposite, arises by and from itself. The singularity of this reality is the nonspecific meaning that is the exaltation of pristine awareness. Pristine awareness arises spontaneously in and as the unitary significance of things. This primordial awareness of pure being suffuses all seemingly concrete phenomena in a unitary cognition. It is vivid direct perception, unthought and unstructured, an open-ended expanse. In the modality of utter purity that is immersed in this perceptual nonduality lies effortless awareness of sameness, the natural equality of all things, and this is the nature of the pure essence of mind.

4

Changeless and unchangeable, there is nothing to desire,
no object of perception, no perceiving mind;
impulsion towards direct self-perception implies fixation on a cause,
but no ultimate equality can come in the bliss of meditation infatuation.

This naturally arising pristine cognition precludes attachment because it has no object within it to grasp and to cling to. In the absence of any object of attachment there is no mind to cling and no mind to grasp and so mind is unlimited. There is only the here-and-now. Subjective and objective factors are resolved in unitary cognition. The unchangeable nature of that awareness is like a timeless, primordial absence of object to be grasped and mind to grasp. If, nevertheless, we are still struck by the imperative to seek and find the nature of mind—that timeless primordial absolute—on a path of direct vivid gnosis, then that implies fixation on a causal path of meditation. Employing such technique, most likely we will become intoxicated and obsessed by the pleasure that arises in the projective function of meditative absorption. In that pleasure-attachment the possibility of attaining the famous sovereign equality is denied.

5

To the one buddha-dimension, all-embracing, nothing can be added,
and since the field of reality is unlimited, it cannot be diminished;
in the reality-display there is no place of heightened mood,
for pleasure resides everywhere equally in the vast self-sprung field.

In this nondual perspective 'the one-buddha dimension' is all-inclusive pure being (dharmakaya), which subsumes the dimensions of clarity (sambhogakaya) and compassion (nirmanakaya). From the beginning it is complete and perfect in itself and nothing can augment or improve it. Likewise, since the reality of self-sprung awareness cannot be reached by movement in any direction, its field of reality is the limitless here and now and cannot, therefore, be circumscribed. Thus, in nondual pure mind experience there is no variation in mood, only the one taste of pure pleasure, for reality is the play of pleasure and the field of reality is the playground of pleasure.

6

*There is no marvelous vision to be seen here with an eye of insight,
and nothing specific to be heard since nothing can be explained;
here the sacred and profane are always inextricably intermingled,
and an ultimate goal, a superior place, cannot be articulated.*

There is no particular understanding or insight to be desired above any other, for all cognition is equal in pure being. There is no particular way of seeing that will provide insight into the here-and-now, for the here-and-now is always present. It is useless to wait to hear something of particular significance because, in the moment, meaning remains unelaborated and cannot be expounded. If the 'sacred', the 'real', is seeming appearance and the 'profane', the 'unreal', is pure fabrication,[9] because verbal expression is an inextricable mixture of these two, it is impossible to articulate the ultimate reality which is, supposedly, a superior state. The ultimate reality of 'absolute emptiness', being expressed and defined, does not exist in reality and cannot be established existentially.

7

*The path of pure mind cannot be conceived as true or false
because self-sprung awareness itself cannot be defined;
in the direct vivid presence of timeless inclusive identity
thought arises but like a shadow.*

Any attempt to determine the manifest pure mind, the appearances that flit across the mind-sky, as real or unreal, authentic or contrived, true or false, is purely academic. Such discussion is informed by mental constructs which cannot comprehend the spontaneous nature of mind. The self-cognizing mind-sky itself surpasses its content. In the freeform identity lacking directed activity, gnosis does not seek to identify itself. In pristine awareness constructs and discursive thoughts are like gossamer shadows without weight or substance. They are the shadow of buddhahood and a shadow is all we can see of it. They are like rainbow-hued figments of mind, neither existent nor nonexistent, neither coming into existence nor ceasing to be.

Every verbal expression in mind or speech is transcended by its nature as the pristine awareness which occurs at one with the verbal formula. Thus the alphabetic glyphs of thought and speech—whether they express positive or negative meanings—are buddha-speech and it is pointless to discuss with oneself the validity of any given experience with a view to any imagined conclusion. Attachment to any particular premise, hypothesis or formula over any other is thereby pre-empted and argument or discussion becomes a dead issue. Every experience is consummate in itself.

8

Its nonexistence is not unqualified—its essence emerges as an absence and its emptiness is not voidness—it is present as empty objects; through recollection of the nature of space, without desire, the pleasure of consummate freeform action is enjoyed and in that untargeted field pristine awareness emerges.

The essence does not exist as any thing, but it emerges as an absence of anything else. Likewise emptiness is not voidness because it is present as an empty field. The 'nonexistence' and 'emptiness' of the pure essence of mind are conceptual tools that deny it substantiality and create an ineffable space in which nonaction and spontaneous creativity occur. 'Absence' or 'nonexistence' describes the source—the pure essence of mind—of a non-objectifiable field or object. 'Emptiness' indicates only the absence of anything concrete or specific in that field and, further, implies the infusion of such an indeterminate reality by a vital fullness. Space is its best analogue and, indeed, by evoking the experience of the nature of space, free of any desire or intention the pure pleasure of pure mind emerges in a freeform field suffused by pristine awareness.

9

The ancient sages, focusing a passionate will,
became utterly lost in the torment of strenuous effort;
the omniscience that is immersion in the natural process,
when articulated, engenders conceptual meditation.

Referring back to the sages of yore,[10] to exemplify a nonproductive, self-defeating mode of meditation, it was not so much the strenuous, passionate, effort that doomed their endeavor but the construction of goals fixed by conceptualizing the undoubted state of omniscience of those who had recognized the true nature of mind. Omniscience is the quality of nonconceptual pristine awareness; when such natural understanding is defined as knowledge of this or that through metaphysical speculation and conceptual fabrication it is turned into a desirable goal and spontaneity is precluded. The rishis pursued a futile temporal path of conceptual goal-oriented meditation.

10

Craving pure pleasure is an attachment sickness;
if it is not cured by the panacea of imperturbable equality,
even the causal bases of higher states are infected by passion.

Desire for happiness or pleasure through meditation is as much an extraneous attachment as desire for sensual pleasure or material objects. Hunger for pure pleasure is chronic heart disease. The universal panacea for desire and attachment is our inborn imperturbable sense of the equality of all experience. Without this natural recognition, desire nullifies even the merit accumulated for the purpose of attaining a higher state of being. Without it, social virtues such as generosity, patience and morality are infected and skewed. So the desire that fuels the ambition to attain a spiritual goal is self-defeating.

Desire in itself is self-liberating, but with craving and addiction— like diseased attachment to the bliss of union—desire becomes a glitch in the process. It is the presence of equality that takes the sting out of desire and allows it spontaneous liberation. Even if it is desire for the virtue creating states of beatitude that is infected by goal-oriented craving, the same applies.

11

Those enmeshed in a negative process by this virulent disease,
aching for progress, are like animals stalking a mirage—
their goal has no existence anywhere in the universe;
even the causal bases of the ten stages obscure the purest mind.

Goal-directed craving entails a negative process that is like pursuing a phantom—the goal is a figment of the imagination and cannot be reached no matter how long the journey. Nirvana can never be reached by striving. The principle applies equally to those seeking a mundane goal as to those who strive to traverse the ten stages of the bodhisattva path—the stages and levels cannot be traversed so long as they are separated from the starting point in the here-and-now where pristine awareness is an immediate source of fulfilment. Even when the goal is one of the ten stages of purification on the bodhisattva path or buddhahood itself, ambition to attain it is a glitch in the natural process.[11]

12

Ultra-fast pristine awareness, beyond thought,
like a spiritual friend—a fountain of gems,
unmotivated, independent of changing circumstance,
by its very nature fulfills all wishes.

Goal-oriented striving is redundant because pristine awareness itself, moving so fast that fulfilment is simultaneous with the need, is totally satisfying. Such pristine awareness is like the wish-fulfilling gem of the masters that is the source of infinite virtue, the precious jewel that we carry in veneration upon our heads. It is like a soul-mate who responds to our unspoken wishes, has no self-directed or ulterior motivation and remains constant in all circumstances whatsoever. It is not something that can be imaged or is contingent upon circumstance. It is gnosis arising from within as our own nature—that is what is totally satisfying.

13

Analyzed it is nothing—letting it be, fine exaltation;
it is truly invisible, yet it gratifies every need:
the master, innocent of self and other, a treasure trove;
the happy isles, revealed in selfless compassion.

This precious wish-fulfilling gem of pristine awareness cannot be examined under the microscope or it appears nonexistent. But naturally relaxing into it, it spontaneously emanates a multiplicity of positive qualities; it is the invisible matrix that emanates all our needs and here the great way is revealed to all. In pristine awareness, where the duality of subject and object, self and other, is resolved, there is the master, the guru-buddha, and the teacher. That is the land of milk and honey, where everything is fulfilled, a field of instantaneous accomplishment. The master is a bodhisattva in his pure land which is an emanation of selfless compassion. This is the emanation body (*tulku*) that never leaves its pure mind source and never becomes a concrete object and this is the wish-fulfilling gem.

14

Unmoving within, it is nothing that can be found within
and turning outside, it cannot be imaged or isolated;
neither extruding nor intruding, this selfless compassion
is inalienable—it abides here timelessly.

This precious jewel of selfless compassion is identical to pure mind and like awakened mind it is said to exist within but cannot be discovered within or indeed anywhere at all. Certainly it cannot be found outside because what appears outside is a projection upon an empty screen and has no substantial reality whatsoever. So this selfless compassion can be neither radiated nor absorbed, neither applied to another nor soaked up from outside, for it cannot move out of its own sphere, which is all-embracing. In no way can it be intentionally or conscientiously applied to an external human or material field or it reduces itself to mawkish pity. It cannot be focused upon a specific target of sympathy. It is a primordial, universal, constant .

15

To yearn for pleasure precludes its dawning—
pleasure is already here, yet still it strains for itself;
in pure delusion we ardently crave nirvana
but such a grasping self has no buddha-vision.

Incessant desire towards a future end frustrates itself because the actual process of desire in this moment is the end itself. Consummation cannot be attained until desire is recognized as the pure pleasure that it always is. The desire for pleasure that looms out of pure mind strains towards what is always ineluctably present in the here-and-now as pure pleasure. In the same way, the desire for nirvana that arises in clouded pristine awareness is consummated only when it recognizes itself as nirvana. So long as it strains towards nirvana the aspiration alienates itself from nirvana and in such a bind the nature of the aspiration as the goal remains obscured. Rather than trying to perform the impossible task of standing aside and admiring pure mind, we jump directly into it!

16

*Where there is no buddha there is no buddha to name
and buddha revealed, to label him is error:
to try to catch buddha 'out there' is a false path
for all things are formless without an iota of substance.*

So long as dualistic perception maintains a gap between desire and pleasure, so-called 'buddha' cannot be seen. In the absence of 'buddha', to employ the concept is to suggest something that does not exist which creates a dichotomy between what is and what might be. To strive for what might be is a chimerical, mistaken quest because 'buddha' has no color or shape and does not exist anywhere. 'Buddha' has no substance or continuity whatsoever, so the label does not refer to any entity or state. Then, when 'buddha' is revealed, there can be no objectification of nondual buddhahood. It cannot be conceptualized and 'he who knows does not speak'. So the word 'buddha' remains phony in any context and whether in a delusive or nondelusive state 'he who speaks does not know'.

17

*Consummate, beyond desire, serene,
insubstantial, and utterly foregone,
the nature of the miraculous ambrosia
does not depend upon any technique.*

The 'miraculous ambrosia' is nondual perception where conscious subject and animate or inanimate object are indissolubly joined in the totality of pristine awareness. This ambrosia (*amrita*) is, therefore, pristine awareness itself which is spontaneously, effortlessly and ineluctably present in every moment. There is no need to apply any technique whatsoever to attain the release and it matters not at all what the shape and color of the immaterial form that is abandoned there. The neurosis of clinging and the pain of attachment is naturally and primordially assuaged.

18

This sublime reality, free and open, all inclusive,
provides recourse for the little ones;
and when concepts dissolve in the vastness
there is no distinction between great and small.

The antidote to the goal-oriented aspirations of adherents to the lesser, causal, levels of Hermits, Disciples and Bodhisattvas, is the vast expanse of naturally perfected reality. In this space all ideas about the nature of reality dissolve, all desire, aspiration and ambition dissolve, all concepts projected upon the sensory fields dissolve. There is only one recourse, technique or antidote, and that is primordial pure mind—which is not to be sought after.

19

Articulated transmission, emergent vision,
which is like an illusionist's trick,
arises in pulsating misty awareness.

Extempore verbalized transmission augmented by secret instruction, or a vision taking momentary form, is like a conjuror's magic, mere illusion. Now you see it; now you don't! It appears to have content but it is utterly insubstantial. Such creativity arises by the power of pristine awareness pulsating in sameness, creating a skein of illusion at each beat, at each beat engulfed in its own purity. Through the self-recognition of ultimate sameness in a torpid mind, pristine awareness is freed from its seeming dullness and cloudiness.

Within seeming delusion pristine awareness emerges spontaneously. In the very process of the volatile fluctuations of delusive energy, in its dispersion and absorption, expansion and contraction, alternating between creative output and ultimately deconstructive rest, in sameness pristine awareness arises. In this way, verbal transmission is the inspired revelation of a dynamic pulsating pristine awareness. Vision arises by the same process. Poetry and art arise likewise. Scripture has the same source. Out of a languid, torpid mind primal awareness shines through and therefore can be said to be the source of spontaneous creativity. This precept is restated in *Pure Golden Ore* verse 5 and *Victory Banner* verse 44.

20

In this universal sovereign approach,
released, accepting, our nature
aspires to nothing and appropriates nothing,
and induces not the slightest presumption.

Self-sufficient we are released from all conceptual supports and mental crutches, free of a spiritual base or port. With presence of equality we are undiscriminating. We have no desires and no needs. The ingenuousness of our pleasure assures that no complacence or arrogance can be generated and this frees us from the seeming womb-like security of the gods. The universality of the process where the upper and lower realms are one, and buddha and sentient beings are indivisible, denies the possibility of the gods' exclusivity as also the sage's divine pride.

21

*As with the soaring garuda in flight
no complication, no simplification,
nothing to lose and nothing to gain.*

The garuda, the mythological king of birds, is egg-born to full maturity and at birth he can glide across the universe with a single movement of his wings. Utterly self-sufficient, fearless, lacking any anxiety, he needs no output or input, radiates nothing and absorbs nothing, without diffusion or concentration, and flying high and free he is completely happy in himself without expectation or trepidation, hope or fear.

22

*That ultimate space, like an ocean,
gives rise to the multiplicity of things;
creative potential, coextensive with space,
is unpredictable in the forms that it takes.*

The ocean is the source of all variety. Still in its depths, its surface spontaneously takes on all peaceful and wrathful forms that represent every kind of human experience. Just as the shape of the ocean's surface is capricious and variable, so the form of creation, the shape of our experience, is changeable, variable and unpredictable. The creativity of the pure essence of mind is all-pervading like space and where it appears to manifest as this or that is always uncertain.

23

*In the pure essence of mind, spontaneously,
ultimate sovereign samadhi arises;
and vision is like a vast ocean,
unstructured, as extensive as space.*

The creative dynamic of the pure essence of mind is ubiquitous although its point of apparent manifestation is uncertain. In every adventitious thought or construct, the ultimate samadhi always arises without concentration or relaxation. With that, then, vision is like a vast ocean or like the sky. Vision has no structure; or it is simultaneously structured and destructured. Thought-free with the sense of equality, it is co-extensive with space. That is the vision.

24

*In this freeform field of Samantabhadra
nothing is born and nothing transforms;
the twelve fold causal chain
denigrates and demeans it.*

In Samantabhadra's field of activity, which is the space of equality, nothing is born and nothing dies, nothing comes into being and nothing ceases to be, so nothing can transform or transmigrate and there is nothing at all that can change. Causality is denied, so there is no karma and no reincarnation. The twelve-fold chain of interdependent origination (ignorance, habitual tendencies, consciousness, name and form, the six sensory fields, contact, feeling, craving, existence, birth, old age and death) is an analysis of samsara, the wheel of life. Entertaining such a theory denigrates and demeans the original buddha, Samantabhadra, by imputing a causal process to what is timeless. Causality precludes the perfection of the here-and-now by the presumption of causes and conditions. It is the premise of an intractable pessimist. But to deny the causal chain diminishes samsara while to affirm it reifies its fleeting appearances—and neither is appropriate to recognition of its nature.

25

*Let the wise recognize the twelve-fold chain
as a door into delusion for the ignorant,
while experience of the six kinds of beings
should be recognized as the primary path.*

If we believe in samsara, affirming the existence of its causes and conditions, a door into samsara's six realms of suffering opens and endless transmigration from realm to realm begins. The ignorant who walk through that door are trapped by delusive appearances. But whoever recognizes the nature of reality understands the twelve links and samsaric appearances as mere concepts and constructs. At the same time, delusory samsaric experience of the six personality types, or six kinds of beings, who populate the six realms of the wheel of life, recognized by the wise as pure mind itself, constitutes the enlightened modality. In this way, what is a trap for those who affirm or deny samsara and its causal analysis is a lucky break for those who understand it as the pure mind process.

26

*Since sensual pursuits are whetted by compassion,
the pleasure of pure mind is enacted in them all;
butchers, whores and taboo-breakers,
unspeakable sinners and outcastes,[12]
all can know nothing but pure pleasure
through inclusive perfection, the nondual elixir.*

When there is no gap between vision and action on the wheel of life, when vision and action are congruent and simultaneous, whatever form the sensory continuum takes, regardless of social opprobrium or taboo, there can only be pure pleasure. In nondual perception the apparent form is always mere gossamer illusion of pure mind. All activity is suffused by compassion for others. This includes the activity of butchers and all erotic indulgence—all is pure mind action and pure pleasure is its inevitable feeling tone. Even the breaking of social taboos is suffused by compassion, regardless of whether it is a single action or lifestyle. The five taboos, or inexpiable crimes, of the Buddhist tradition, are matricide, killing an arhat, patricide, creating schism in the community and letting the blood of a *tathagata* with malice—these actions are said to result in immediate rebirth in hell without a moment for absolution. The elixir of nonduality absolves, absolutely, all guilt and in ultimate equality there can only be pure pleasure.[13]

27

This unstructured, unthought, pure essence of mind
cannot be hidden in the continuum of mind:
for indiscriminate pure mind yogis
pure mind is present in every situation.

Our actual identity, being all-inclusive, perfect and complete, our identity as pure mind, is inseparable from pure pleasure. It is known as 'the inconceivable essence'. It is not something discrete concealed somewhere in the continuity of being, or in the personality. It is there for everybody to see in every situation that arises. As we act without discrimination, neither rejecting nor adopting whatever arises, it is implicit in the sense of total fulfilment. Nothing lacking, nothing superfluous, it resides in the absence of motivation. It is the equanimity that exists in experience of the thing-in-itself, the essence of unstructured experience. It exists as the nature of mind in the continuity of thought.

Pure Golden Ore

Just as ore is suffused by pure gold so all experience is pervaded by pure mind. The ore, indeed, is as good as gold. Experience of all things composed of the five elements is thus the pure mind teacher. Here Samantabhadra transmits the heart meaning of that axiom. Natural nonaction is the theme and nonmeditation is the mode. Manjushri, the Gentle Virgin Prince, is evoked as the exemplar of this unequivocating transmission. The yogin rests naturally in the spontaneous pleasure of effortless perfection![14]

Hey, Magnificent Being, listen!

1   Pure Mind is the Light of Buddha and the Heart of All Things

Pure mind, inexpressible, beyond ideation,
as the light of the teacher is extolled by all;
as the heart of experience it is the Gentle Prince
resting in the spontaneous pleasure of effortless perfection.

In the pure essence of mind a samadhi exists that transcends the entire field of ideas and is beyond expression. Resting in the samadhi that is beyond mentation, all buddha perceives the pure essence of mind as the light that is the teacher, the Lamp of the Buddha, and praise it. It is the core of everything, all phenomena and all revelation, where everything is known. This omniscience is personified as the Gentle Youth, shining in glory. He has no goal to attain and nothing to strive for, so in him nonaction is effortlessly perfected and without any endeavor he rests in the matrix of pure pleasure.

2   The Pure Mind Modality is Not Conditional Upon A Vow of Moral Conduct

As the basis of all disciplines, such as moral conduct,
pure mind provides release in its every mode,
it is buddha's mother and the universal path—
without it no buddha could come into being:
I am the way of supreme liberation.

The pure essence of mind is the foundation of a vast array of behavioral modes, including the disciplines derived from the vow of moral conduct and from the tantric commitments. Insofar as pure mind is the ground of them all, all of them partake of its liberating function. The pure essence is thus called 'the mother of joyful buddha'. The all-inclusive path, however, embraces everybody whether or not they maintain vows of moral conduct. If vows of moral conduct lack the modality of release, no buddha would be begotten; but whatever the nature of the conduct since it is grounded in the pure essence of mind it possesses the function of release. For this reason, there is no vow of moral conduct in the modality of supreme liberation. It is this freedom that Vajrasattva represents.

The pure essence of mind, as the supreme source, is the origin of all the paths and approaches to buddhahood, and provides simultaneously the process of release of all those manifold lifestyles. Vajrasattva is the modality of supreme liberation (see *Victory Banner* verse 1). All disciplines and samaya commitments whatsoever are assimilated to these aspects of buddhahood and thus subsumed by Vajrasattva. The process of supreme release, however, is dependant upon no discipline or samaya commitment whatsoever.

3   The Universal Process of Liberation Inherent in Pure Mind is Inscrutable

Subtle and elusive, this universal path transcends thinking and nonthinking;
without location or reference—indeterminate—it is beyond all ideation;
unutterable, it has no color or shape in a sensory field;
intangible and inscrutable, it is inexpressible.

The universal process of liberation inherent in pure mind cannot be conceived and transcends thought and thoughtlessness. It has no reference point in any concrete name or form; it cannot be isolated or localized in any way. It is utterly indeterminable and thus cannot be framed as any idea and cannot be expressed verbally. In this way it is subtle and elusive.

4   The Dangers of the Path of Formal Meditation

Whoever follows the ancient sages' path
becomes sick from attachment to the meditation process;
his teachers' literal instruction construed as a quest
he chases a stream of concepts, as if pursuing a mirage:
the perfect modality cannot be indicated by words
and any 'true doctrine' is a travesty of Vajrasattva.

Whether Buddhist, Hindu or Bon, the classical path of meditation is a snare and a delusion when attachment to it becomes obsessive and it becomes an end in itself. The habit of meditation becomes a disease when there is no liberating function in the process. It is a disease when a blissful trance state seemingly separates an arrogant yogin from his mind. But above all it is a disease simply because it is goal-oriented and promises attainment only if the present is prostituted to the future. This state of alienation is caused by mistaking mental constructs for the path, to mistake the shadow of the meaning expressed in words for the thing itself.

The meanings of the words are taken as sacred concepts. The letter of the instruction is taken to heart rather than the spirit. To take the teacher's word literally is, for example, to construe reality as something concrete to be attained by striving in technique and method rather than as a door into the reality of the moment. Words and concepts are a means to their own transcendence in the here-and-now. Fascination with structure is a deviation; doctrine professed as 'true' and 'correct' gives Vajrasattva a mask of the ridiculous.

5   Bewilderment and Ignorance Are the Ground of Enlightenment

Purity and impurity, as one, indissolubly mixed,
pristine awareness and bewilderment are indivisible;
this is the lamp of unimpeded clarity free of mentation
and intractable nescience, in itself, is sovereign samadhi.

All the polarities and dichotomies perpetrated by the intellect are resolved in the timeless pristine awareness of pure mind. What is called 'pure' and what is called 'impure' are a seamless whole, and what is called 'pristine awareness' and what is called 'bewilderment' and 'ignorance' are precisely the same thing. Both ignorance and pristine awareness reside in pure mind and the nature of mind is the nature of all. This unity is the lamp of buddha and the heart of pure mind, and pristine awareness itself is by definition unimpeded and all-penetrating. The state of unmitigated gloom is inherently a state of supreme absorption so that 'stupidity' and 'languid indifference' are another way of saying 'undiscriminating samadhi'. (See also *Great Garuda* verse 19 and *Victory Banner* verse 44.)

6   There is Nothing to See with the Buddha-eye

The eye of direct insight seeing directly sees nothing
and it is called 'the buddha-eye of omniscience';

*know the nature of vastness without center or boundary
and there lies undiscriminating sovereign equality.*

In the samadhi of pristine awareness there are no points of reference, no image to focus upon, no particularity. 'The buddha-eye of omniscience' sees directly into the nature of things and because that reality has no field of reference it is said to see nothing or not to see at all. A 'soft' expanse without center or circumference is a definition of reality.

7 Whatever Appears to the Senses is Pure Enjoyment

*Pure mind and its habits are one, indissolubly mixed:
all manifest experience, by mind projected,
shines as adornment neither accepted nor rejected—
simply let it be and enjoy it!*

In the pure essence of mind, in the natural condition, there is no distinction between mind and its proclivities. So there is no chance to modify or change habits. Whatever appears in the windows of mind—the five sensory windows—is determined by mental habit and constructed by the conditioned mind. But the senses themselves make no distinction between the forms that appear in these windows. They make no judgment of quality or suitability. There is no attribution of good or bad. They do not suppress or reject some forms while letting others in. The indiscriminate senses allow each sensation to arise as aesthetic decoration to be enjoyed in and as itself, regardless of its form. There is absolutely nothing to be done to it. Any intention to change it or modify it precludes the pure enjoyment.

8 No Vice is Outside the Pale of Pure Mind

*Activity that is anathema or taboo,
the five emotions and the five inexpiable crimes,*

on the path of purity deliver sovereign equality;
nothing is rejected, not even sex.

Insofar as proclivities of mind that spontaneously manifest as conventionally repugnant anti-social activity or as passionate emotivity are inseparable from pure mind, they generate experience not different from any ordinary activity. But since they are accompanied by social disdain, and perhaps personal guilt, they provide a space of alienation in which the equality of pristine awareness being imperative to sanity is seemingly amplified. In such experience, without seeking to cultivate or abandon it, lies sublime and utter purity and whoever enters there attains the ultimate equality of pure mind. Thus the abodes of desire—in particular the opposite sex—are not to be avoided. This is highlighted in the mahayoga samaya commitments.

Although social taboos vary from society to society passionate emotivity is universally of five kinds—lustful, angry, jealous, arrogant and fearful. The five inexpiable crimes are matricide, patricide, arhaticide, creating schism in the community and maliciously drawing the blood of a buddha, none of which, it is said, can be absolved because the karmic consequences are immediate.

9   The Traditionalist Approaches Are Anathema

The intellect conditioned by traditional form and meaning,
the three samadhis set, following doctrine and dogma,
this is a glitch in the effortless transmission—it is delusion;
abide in the spontaneous pleasure of free-form perfection![15]

We know history by the forms that tradition passes to us through body language, signs and symbols, by oral or bardic transmission and through books. We also know it by primordial intuition of Samantabhadra and Vajrasattva. When this legacy of tradition is assimilated to the rational mind, tested and proven, when 'history' is spun out into a linear, logical pattern through time by intellectual endeavor, the yogin becomes conditioned to the forms and meanings of the tradition and loses all spontaneity. If the history of philosophy, likewise, discerned in the strata of veils that enshroud momentary pure being, becomes a function of linear logical mind, conditioned by the academic approach it is delusory. If, meanwhile, he practices the three mahayoga samadhis of 'body', 'speech' and 'mind' with meditative absorption, he cultivates the three modes or dimensions of being (*trikaya*) on a path with a goal in mind. (The three mahayoga samadhis of the here-and-now, the all-illuminating samadhi and the seed syllable samadhi, relate respectively to the three dimensions of essence, nature and compassion.) Through projection and application of the gender principles of means and insight, he is lost on a goal-oriented path. Following the established tenets of dogma and doctrine, he may engage in comparative philosophy and even speculative metaphysics, he may even teach it, but he is lost in goal-directed endeavor. This method of traditionalist scholars and conventional intellectuals effectively blankets the momentary effusion of Samantabhadra's spontaneous transmission. Imperative freeform nonaction is lost in the straight-jacket of tradition and goal-oriented discipline.

10 Nonaction is the Natural Condition

The core of sublime self-sprung awareness,
imperturbable, unchanging, unelaborated—
this is the ambrosia of timeless consummation
that vanquishes the pain of any exertion:
every ambition fulfilled, rest in the here-and-now!

The nature of cognition itself is ultimately fulfilling and forestalls the need to strive for any satisfaction through the strenuous exertion of directed activity. The suffering of failure to obtain what is desired, of obtaining what is undesirable and of losing what is in hand is all obviated by the elixir of pristine awareness. Since pristine awareness cannot be changed, the here-and-now is perfect and complete in itself. Even if there is an illusion of evolution, the actuality of the moment is beyond change, so there is no goal to be achieved and nothing to do. The ambrosia of nonduality consummates the activity of every moment: nonaction is the mode in a field of effortless consummation.

Hey, Magnificent Being, listen!
All and everything in experience
has the nature of pure mind—
it is the seminal nucleus;
incapable of elaboration or concentration,
expansion or contraction,
origination or cessation,
unconfined, it is simply being.
This inconceivable essence,
timelessly present like the sky,
ubiquitous like space,
transcends ideas and speech.[16]

The Eternal Victory Banner: The Vast Space of Vajrasattva

The Eternal Victory Banner is the source of all transmission and pith instruction. More specifically, it teaches total nonaction whereby all and everything is already perfected. In this great transmission, Samantabhadra reveals himself to Vajrasattva as his own nature. 'I am you,' he affirms. 'I am pure mind and pure mind is the vast space of Vajrasattva.'[17]

The Timeless Moment of Reality

1

The vast space of Vajrasattva
the all-good expanse of the field of reality,
this is the all-releasing and pure modality
uncreated, unceasing and unthinking.

The Sublime Teacher—Samantabhadra:
Vajrasattva is the all-pervasive spaciousness of our unchanging being whose exaltation lies in his unalterable self-sprung awareness. His undiscriminating reality is Samantabhadra, the all-good, all-inclusive field of reality, the dharmadhatu. Everything dissolving into it and emerging from it in unimpeded and relaxed enjoyment, all buddha and sentient beings of the three-fold universe (sensual, aesthetic and formless) are released instantaneously into pure mind. In this way, no substantial field of reality is ever created, nothing whatsoever ever comes into existence or ceases to be. Self-sprung awareness lies therein,

unimpeded, in a relentless samadhi that has no beginning nor end, conceiving nothing nor motivating anything at all.

Samantabhadra, who is pure mind itself, is the perfect teacher of every situation. Disclosing his nature to Vajrasattva, he says, 'You are the clear sky of pure awareness and I, as the teacher, show you my undiscriminating reality. I am pure mind and all and everything simultaneously emanates from me and dissolves into me and in that process lies ineluctable release.'[18]

Thus the reality of the teacher, Vajrasattva, is the nature of being.

2

Loving kindness is already consummate
so compassion is not pursued;
supremely vast and deep
no quality exists to acclaim.

The Exaltation of Enlightenment Here and Now:
Loving kindness is the nature of the all-pervasive pure mind, so it is love itself that has already fulfilled the ultimate goal which is the ever-immanent reality of Vajrasattva. Compassion is then the nature of reality, as buddha affirms, and it is futile to focus and direct to any being what is already present as his or her nature. It is impossible to cultivate what is naturally, already fully potentiated and so any practice of compassion is redundant. It is counter-productive to allow compassion to become an affective response to extraneous pain, since that would create a dichotomy of inner and outer and an obstacle to spontaneous compassionate flow.

The exaltation of pristine awareness is its immaculate nature and this can be neither improved nor altered nor conscientiously cultivated nor actualized. Such exaltation is profound because dualistic perception is transcended. In that ulterior nonreferential space where there is no imperfection or blemish, there is no fault to rectify, and no flaw to acknowledge, so how can there be any particular quality to extol or any success to celebrate?[19]

Thus Vajrasattva is shown as loving kindness.

3

Intentions unstirring from their own nature,
through nonaction are released and activate release;
unseeking self-sprung awareness,
liberating, reveals the process of release.

Transmission Ultimately Resolving All Experience:
Our identity—our individuality—is the unalterable reality of pure mind. Even our intentions and impulses, our aims and objectives, our reactions and responses, can never escape their natural condition which is this unalterable reality. By doing nothing at all, through no directed activity, free of endeavor, without striving—which is nonaction—the Great Perfection is recognized. Pristine awareness, contingent upon neither cause nor condition, liberates itself through its ungrasping natural state, and reveals the liberating process.

To resolve all experience as pure meaning is the purpose of the essential message of the transmission of the *Eternal Victory Banner*: release into the great perfection is inherent in every movement of the mind, whether of a buddha or ordinary being, so long as there is no striving to attain it.[20]

Thus the ordinary mind is naturally liberated in the moment. The character and personality are never divorced from pure mind.

The Timeless Moment of Intrinsic Gnosis

4

Vajrasattva is the great elements
intrinsically present in all beings;
even though false notions obsess us,
release is self-sprung—but only in him.

The Consummation of Mahayoga:
The totality, Vajrasattva, is universally present as the five 'great' elements of earth, water, fire, air and space, and these elements are the five all-creating buddhas. All the six kinds of beings—gods, men, titans, hungry ghosts, animals and hell-beings—are composed of these elements. Thus Vajrasattva is a constant, all-embracing presence. We may conceive of the elements in any way—symbolically, personified, materialistically, or functionally—but regardless of any such notions and despite any conceptualization of Vajrasattva, as the five buddhas he is the place of ineluctable, spontaneous release.

In mahayoga the five elements are located in the mindstream and visualized as the mandala of the five buddhas (Vairochana, Akshobhya, Ratnasambhava, Amitabha and Amoghasiddhi) representing the primordial purity of the five elements. This is a contrived process of goal-oriented meditation. But since the pure mind-stream is the great perfection it encompasses all such enumerations and all such meditative techniques and the moment of praxis arises spontaneously as Vajrasattva. Mahayoga provides a door into the great perfection itself when its meditative technique is recognized as embraced by pure mind.[21]

Thus Vajrasattva is intrinsically, naturally present in the here-and-now.

The Timeless Moment of Natural Exaltation

5

Exalted pristine awareness, so elusive,
can be accomplished through means and insight;
though these appear as a supporting extraneous fiction,
real pleasure arises only spontaneously.

The Consummation of Anuyoga:
Pristine awareness is impossible to locate because it has no reference, no address. The difficulty of access may be overcome through recognition of the intrinsic union of reality and gnosis. This would appear to imply a dependence upon an ineffectual nominal duality, but since the exaltation of pristine awareness—immediate pure pleasure—arises only from and in pure mind, which is quite beyond cause and effect, its nature can only be spontaneity.

In the case of intractable ignorance of the intrinsic perfection of the nature of mind where pristine awareness remains elusive, recourse may be made to the anuyoga construct of means and insight which provides a referential address to the pure pleasure of pristine awareness. Skillful means is gnosis (iconographically represented as Samantabhadra, the male principle) and insight is the field of reality (Samantabhadri, the female principle). Pure pleasure is intrinsic to this timeless primordial union and spontaneity is its nature. Anuyoga is fulfilled through the great perfection of mind.

All the skillful means of the lower, secondary, approaches to mahabodhi arise out of the pure nature of mind, which is perfect and complete in itself and can never be divorced from the gnosis of natural spontaneity. Here Dzogchen is the complete yoga, subsuming all others (see also verse 52).

Thus the intrinsical vast gnosis of pure mind is shown to encompass the apparent duality of the gender principles of means and insight.

The Timeless Unsought Moment

6

The sublime magical illusion is easy to find:
through a subtle understanding of actuality,
of all potential and potency,
it immediately emerges by itself.

The Consummation of Sattva-yoga:
Sublime magical illusion, the display of *maya*, is self-revealing pure mind. When its nature is understood as uncreated and unstructured, as a totally insubstantial illusion, like a conjurors trick, it is reflexively attained. Out of the realization of its nature as uncontrived reality, the indestructible potential of pure being and pristine awareness, the vast potential of buddha past, present and future emerges smoothly without any obstruction as all and everything. The sense of illusion cannot be forced; it is reflexive and innate and cannot be separated from a realization of suchness, the field of reality.

The vision of illusionary reality is a spontaneous revelation that cannot be forced. Nevertheless, this natural process is facilitated in outer yogatantra (*sattva-yoga*). The process involves visualization of the qualities of a buddha-deity (*jnana-sattva*) and subsequent internalized identification of that as the commitment-being (*samaya-sattva*). Perception of magical illusion arises spontaneously in that practice. But such meditation is child's play (in verse 36).

In this verse and the next it is shown that making any effort, any attempt to find the illusive nature of reality, is futile and counterproductive. There is nothing to do!

7

The invisible nature of reality
fills the mind when searching stops;
stressing about the what and the wherefore
inhibits its spontaneous arising.

The Fulfilment of Nonmeditation:
The delusion of a material environment and the existence of animate beings cannot arise in the perceptual nonduality of pure mind. This reality is an absence of appearances. Simply by relaxing, unstressed, wanting nothing—which is the supreme meditation of nonmeditation—there it is! The attempt to pin down essentially nonexistent appearances, to insist upon something concrete where nothing substantial exists, to seek any definitive meaning: this is similar to trying to put a solid roof on an imaginary house. Nothing can come of nothing.

Thus searching for something that is already there and the counter-result of anxious striving is futile.

The Inexpressible Timeless Moment

8

This hermetically sealed reality[22]
cannot be transmitted to the ear;
and neither has the tongue the power
to express a tit of it.

The Exaltation of Nonenlightenment:
The teaching of all-inclusive perfection cannot be expressed by buddha or man or woman and so it cannot be transmitted orally. If it cannot be spoken or heard, it does not exist. So what is enlightenment?

Buddhahood or enlightenment is unattainable and its reality cannot be taught or expressed. It is beyond mentation, nonreferential, indeterminable, lacks any indication and is noncomposite. In this sense it does not exist; it is an absence, and in this vast absence lies its exaltation. Nonenlightenment translates as universal enlightenment.

Thus there is no such thing as enlightenment.

The Timeless Moment of Immunity to Karma

9

The suffering of beings is bodhichitta,
yet fully awakened, it is song and dance;
unstirring, immovable,
like infinite space, it is sameness.

Pith Instruction on Pure mind:
The pain of each of the six kinds of beings—human beings, gods, titans, hungry ghosts, animals and devils—is determined by a particular emotional (hormonal) poison, and all of it is the essence of pure mind. Since it is all-pervading, pure mind comprehends all pain through the empty dimensions of physical, energetic and mental emanation, and thereby it is recognized as the wonderful display of pure being and manifold pristine awareness of buddha past, present and future. The activity of all beings, forever spontaneously arising, the pernicious reactivity of desire, aversion,

stupidity, jealousy, pride and greed, all spontaneously arising forever, all emerges in and is comprehended by the pure essence of mind. It can never become anything but pure mind. Because pure mind has the nature of equality, it suffuses all human suffering and activity equally, just as infinite space permeates all things. (See also verses 15 and 16.)

Human beings can never be 'cooked' by karma—never need be slaves to karma. Pure mind renders karmic conditioning ineffective and impotent. Karma is denied here as anything but delusory construct of the intellect, karmic product accepted as the illusory basis of the primary Dzogchen method. *Experience of the six kinds of beings, should be recognized as the primary path* (p. 25). The all-suffusing gnosis of pure mind, however, overwhelms karma, rendering it redundant. Karma is, after all, mere imputation.[23]

Thus the wheel of life arises out of pure mind and always remains pure mind.

10

We tend to interpret congruous distinctions
as 'karmic' relationship;
inasmuch as 'karma' holds sway
self-sprung awareness is lacking.

Perfection Unconditioned by Karma:
All buddha's pure pleasure, and the pain and anxiety of ordinary people's passions, are identical as the essence of pure mind. Yet our equivocal intellect persists in explaining the apparent discrepancy between buddha and sentient beings, and the differences in people's behavior, by reference to the effects of previous action and we become enmeshed in a web of mental constructs created by linear, causal thought processes. Thus, belief

in karma is like an overpowering drug that clouds the mind and inhibits the emergence of pristine awareness. Free of all causes and conditions pristine awareness arises spontaneously.

Thus it is affirmed that belief in karma is an obstacle to the spontaneous emergence of pristine awareness. The intellect seeks to concretize distinctions and reify illusion by substantiating causal relationship. But thought cannot stir the reality-field.

11

The sole cause, as the immutable condition,
never originating can never be destroyed;
in this timeless primordial pure essence of mind,
speculative thought-forms cannot affect the reality-field.

Perfection Without Recourse:
Pure mind is the universal source, the first cause, the only condition. Like the vajra it is immutable and all-victorious. Since it has neither cause nor seed, it is not created; because it has no external condition acting upon it, it is indestructible. This timeless pure essence of mind is immune to mental constructs that seek to condition the mind to causality. Even the most intense speculative thought and potent ideas that seek to structure it, explain it, divulge it, alter it or pin it down, remain mere fluff in the mind and the field of reality remains unmoving.

Thus it is emphasized that karma is a concept imposed upon immaculate uncaused reality and like any thought-form is ineffectual in altering the natural perfection of the pure mind reality in any way. Karmic patterning, as mental construct, is ineffective.

The Timeless Moment of Mental Effort

12

*Concentration in its finest form
in its very nature is nonreflective;
as unreflected, unaltered experience,
in thought itself, pristine awareness arises.*

The Glitch of Concentrated Absorption:
Nonmeditation includes and transcends all positive and negative veils, even the obscuring trance-qualities that arise in meditative absorption. These trance-qualities, including imperturbability, clarity, bliss, serenity, resplendence, pristine awareness suffusing mind, and extra-sensory perception, become glitches and veils only when they are objectified. But the natural concentration inherent in meditative absorption is free of perceptual dualism and automatically subsumes these trance-qualities. This finest, natural concentration is nonreflective and incapable of ideation. So why strive to attain thoughtlessness? In the nonmeditation of natural concentration, discursive thought itself, left alone, unaltered, effloresces as pristine awareness. In the simple natural state of concentration that is unthought and thoughtless, the nature of emergent thought is pristine awareness itself. Naturally perfect meditation—nonmeditation—is free of all motivation and mental striving. Pristine awareness arises in thought itself, thus meditative absorption is redundant.

Glitches in the Dzogchen modality are a function of a delusive dualism that produces mental effort. While the slightest endeavor in the face of a complete absence of motivation and striving in pure mind is folly, nevertheless that folly is naturally pure and perfect in itself and arises in a timeless moment of mental exertion.[24]

Thus thought and mental constructs themselves are pristine awareness.

13

Some identify pure mind as a subtle door:
seeking a way to isolate it
they fixate on the voidness of the mindstream—
if it is contrived it is conceptual meditation.

The Glitch of Subtle Method:
There is no perceptual dualism in nonmeditation, but within the consciousness that constructs subjective and objective elements in sensory perception pure mind can be conceived as the door of liberation—something infinitely subtle but still concrete. In a dualistic frame, pure mind is thus regarded as an entrance into a higher state and not the starting point, the path and the goal rolled into one. Based on such an idea, in physical isolation, free of intrusive energy forms, meditation becomes a method of putting the sensory fields and mental activity into abeyance through a very fine samadhi of voidness. When the chakras of 'body', 'speech' and 'mind' are visualized in such meditation techniques they also are subtly concretized. Such technique is always contrived and goal-oriented in nature. Any meditation that involves intellectual activity, such as focusing on a particular aspect of mind or a visualization, however subtle, and any meditation that can be deconstructed, is conceptual in nature.[25]

Thus pure mind, which lacks any impulse to seek itself, inveigles itself into subtle meditative endeavor.

14

Some believe that by designating cause and effect,
both virtue and vice are clearly defined
and the mundane world is transcended:
moral discrimination is supreme presumption!

The Glitch of Moral Discrimination:
To designate moral cause and effect is to create a self-contained and self-fulfilling system of behavior and reward. What is defined as virtue invariably produces a positive result and what is defined as vice a negative result. In this life the happiness of heaven and the upper realms is the effect of virtuous behavior and the misery of hell and the lower realms is the result of vicious activity. Through the moral discipline of cultivating virtuous activity and forsaking vice the suffering of the world is transcended.

Familiar with the moral causal process and skilled in the discipline of moral discrimination the result of any action can be predicted; but this facility may produce enormous complacency and arrogance that can result in exclusivity and intolerance. As a solution to the problem of existence, furthermore, this analysis is incompatible with the pure mind modality, wherein the conception and consonant action are simultaneous, the conception, anyway, consisting of pure mind reality and the action as nonaction. There is no duality of cause and effect in pure mind.

The path of moral conduct as a method of liberation is contrary to the pure mind principle of nonaction and absence of endeavor. Goal-oriented purveyors of karmic cause and effect entrap themselves in exclusive complacency. Yet thought itself is pristine awareness.

Thus this verse shows that even moralists are encompassed by the great perfection.

The Timeless Moment of Seamless Nonduality

15

The words 'attachment' and 'detachment',
as in the middle way, are but echo,
and pleasure and pain are basically the same.
The Lord of Beings, Vajrasattva, said that.

Unequivocal Congruence of Pleasure and Pain:
Desire focuses upon an imaged object in the sensory fields, where attachment arises. But since the sensory fields have no substance and can be said to have no existence, desire and attachment have no real objective. In this sense neither attachment nor detachment are real; they appear only as indices in mere word play. In the middle way all sound is but echo, and investigating 'attachment' and 'detachment' as mere sound, both are similar music to the ear.

Furthermore, the reality of pleasure and pain, happiness and suffering, and the five passions, are identical in the pure essence of mind. Here 'identity' means causal identity, which in the Dzogchen context means their real identity in and as pure mind; the labels 'pleasure' and 'pain' refer to their nominal distinction in dualistic perception. Vajrasattva is sovereign lord of the six kinds of beings of the six realms insofar as he is the nature of the elements that compose them (see verses 4 and 46).[26]

Thus the great perfection is seamless and flawless in nondual vision.

The Timeless Moment of Self-sprung Awareness

16

Vajrasattva says:
Desire, anger and bewilderment
also occur in the sublime pure mind process;
and the five sensual pleasures
ornament the field of reality.

Exaltation of the Enlightened Field of Reality:
The reality of pure mind is the field of reality of Samantabhadra, the dharmadhatu. The potential pollutants on the pure mind path are desire, hatred and bewilderment; these three tendencies—positive, negative and neutral—are immediately integrated into enlightened existential reality through the buddha-modes of 'body', 'speech' and 'mind' respectively. The five sensual pleasures of our usual behavior—sight, sound, smell, taste and tactile sensation—most potent in sensual-sexual situations, are then adornments of the field of reality, like small baskets of flowers tossed onto the surface of a stream. They are instantaneously integrated as pure being and pristine awareness. In this way indulgence in sensual pleasure is the pure mind process itself and enjoyment is its mode.

Pristine awareness arises spontaneously in desire, aversion and bewilderment (objects of the internal senses), and also in the five sensual pleasures (the objects of the five external senses). Thus the field of reality is always enlightened (see also verse 44). The exaltation of the field of reality as already enlightened is elaborated in terms of Vajrasattva as the five great elements in verses 4 and 47.

Thus passion and sensual pleasure are the path.

17

The concept of space is unoriginated,
the concept itself the same as space;
in the detachment of dedicated space
ultimate self-validating space emerges.

The Reality of Dzogchen Anuyoga:
The reality of anuyoga is the vajra-sensory fields. The thought of space, like space itself, has no substance or origin and is, therefore, said to be unoriginated and unstructured and that is the nature of the field of reality. Constructs and concepts—all thought-forms—arise in the mind-sky like clouds or miasma. Their particularity never comes into existence. They remain utterly without structure, as is the nature of the field of reality. Concepts are therefore like space. Like concepts, the five sensual pleasures—form, sound, smell, taste and touch—are seen as neutral, desire-free space and through the idea that everything is space, all-inclusive spaciousness, thick with meaning, emerges.

There can be no attachment to conceptualized pure being (dharmakaya) due to its illusory spacious nature. All concepts are dedicated as space, but conceptual pure being in particular—the pure being of 'body', 'speech' and 'mind', and 'past', 'present' and 'future'—seen as space, the reality of pure being is realized as self-validating space which is the ultimate purpose. This is an analysis of a spontaneous, instantaneous process.

Here the process wherein the six sensory fields are recognized as the reality of pure mind—vajra-sensory field—is described. This recognition is accomplished by their 'dedication' as space. Here dedication means the projection of the idea of space upon constructs arising in the sensory fields and thereby actualizing their inherent spacious reality. It describes thought-forms and sensual pleasure arising spontaneously as pristine awareness.

There is no gap between the intention and the action. The process occurs within the spontaneity of self-sprung awareness. The notion of 'dedication' assigns this momentary reality to anuyoga.[27]

Thus recognition of the spaciousness of concepts actuates the great perfection.

The Timeless Moment of Union with the Consort

18

Unthought sameness, pure being,
like the moon's reflection in water, cannot be grasped;
in the all-good display of Samantabhadra
it is revealed as the ulterior vowels and consonants.

The Perfection of Samantabhadra's Display:
The reality of pure mind is like space, and mind, unthinking and without constructs, is the sameness of pure being (dharmakaya). Within pure being actuality lacks any concrete name or form whatsoever—it is utterly insubstantial—so there is nothing to grasp and hold on to. Within the unoriginated pure being of Samantabhadra the magical illusion of creation is apparent and all of creation is Samantabhadra's display. In as much as this display of reality is like the reflection of the moon in water it cannot be grasped. That is the reality of immediate phenomenal manifestation.

The phantasmagoria of Samantabhadra's display is a revelation of an interior language. The vowels of this language represent its unborn, unstructured nature, the consonants gnosis which can never be crystalized. The intermingling of vowels and consonants in a moment of nondual experience of the totality is called union with the *mudra* or consort. The union of the reality of pure mind (the vowels) and gnosis (the consonants) is primordial and timeless—there is no method or technique to facilitate it. In the anuyoga of the previous verse, this union is to be recognized in the spaciousness of concepts as well as sensual pleasure.[28]

Thus the unity of language and the form of the magical display is revealed.

19

As the A and the adorning TA,
as the PA and its complex elaborations,
in the field of experience of the finite world
ulterior buddha-speech emerges.

Direct Transmission—Emanation in the Nature of Mind:
Samantabhadra's pure being (dharmakaya) in pure mind reality (dharmadhatu) is defined by the glyph A, which is pure potential, and the glyph TA, which is the potentiation. The glyph PA describes the entire elaborate miraculous emanation within pure being. The aggregates of this magical display are the subjective functions of mind (name and form, feeling, perception, volition and consciousness). The eight forms of consciousness (five sensory and three mental) are secondary emanations that embrace the entire field of multifarious experience of the finite world. Within that field, the five sensual pleasures of the five emotions are the energy patterns of buddha past, present and future, and they are known as buddha-speech. Thus the uncreated pure mind reality of form, sound, smell and so on, is ulterior buddha-speech, just because it is uncreated.

'Buddha-speech' may be interpreted as vibration or as energy patterns, but in this description of the process of emanation within pure being, such energy constellations are formalized as alphabetic glyphs. The glyph PA is the first letter of the word 'padma', the embryonic sound, the generative organ. Out of PA arise the vowels and consonants each corresponding to an aspect of emanation—the five aggregates, the eight types of consciousness, the five emotions, the five sensual pleasures, etc.—and in the complexity of sensual, aesthetic and formless experience in the field of reality they spell the whole gamut of possible activity. Since the reality of sensual pleasure is unborn it is the ulterior voice of the buddha. Since reality is unborn the content of the moment is buddha-teaching.

Aspects of emanation consist of the five aggregates (name and form, sensation, feeling, volition and consciousness), the eight types of consciousness (consciousness of the five external and three internal senses), the five emotions (desire, anger, pride, jealousy and fear), the five sensual pleasures (sight, sound, taste, touch and sensation), the five sense fields, etc.

Thus union with the consort is described.

20

No! the field of buddha-experience
cannot be found by seeking and striving;
since as sixfold experience it is no field
to seek it is like a blind man reaching for the sky.

The Glitch of Striving:
A serious deviation from Dzogchen praxis is to search for what is spontaneously and ineluctably present. Pure being and pristine awareness that comprise the marvelous field of buddha-experience are contingent upon nothing. The field itself is instantaneously self-sprung. Any attempt to grasp the desirable and fascinating objects of the senses is bound to be frustrated because nothing substantial is there. The impulse to reach out to

grasp the six objects of consciousness (that comprise 'sixfold experience') derives from a delusive perceptual dualism. It is as futile and foolish as a blind man stretching up his arms in order to grasp the sky.

Thus there is danger in striving for a product. To do so is an error in behavior. The union with the consort (the field of buddha-experience) is naturally perfected in the here-and-now and no technique or effort can facilitate it.

21

The path of purity reaching from height to height
is at odds with the freeform process;
journeying on the pathless path,
as in boundless space, there is no destination.

The Glitch of Belief in Progress on a Path:
The yogin who believes that the path of buddha, the pure mind process, is a graduated path, is sidetracked onto a structured path of levels and stages. There are no stages in the Dzogchen process; there are no degrees of attainment. A graduated path of purification is incompatible with effortless spontaneity in which there is nothing to do; this is the path of imperative nonaction. Utter relaxation on an unstructured path does not allow for striving towards a structured goal. Progress on the Dzogchen path is an endless process and if there were any destination it would be the ever-receding horizon. On a graduated path the converse is true: each moment is the destination and there is no other goal.

Thus to deviate from the pure mind modality to a graduated path is a potential error.

The Timeless Moment of Complete Perfection

22

*Because things are perfect just as they are,
in the moment of revelation lies the attainment;
the essence of pure mind is the universal source
and the entire reality pure and simple. Marvelous!*

The Aural Transmission:
Things are pure and simple just as they are because in the all-good, immutable reality of Samantabhadra there is no such thing as evolution, development or progress. Only the one reality is continuously present. Whatever appears momentarily in the mind-sky is the complete goal, the ultimate totality.

In the modality of oral transmission whatever is taught and revealed in the moment is ineluctably realized in the moment by whoever is capable. The attainment is intrinsic to the momentary efflorescence, and the revelation and attainment are simultaneous in the same way that the pure essence of mind is at once indeterminate reality itself and the source of reality.

Thus the moment is totally perfect and complete and source and reality have a supra rational identity. This and the following two verses treat complete perfection, all-inclusive intrinsic perfection of the here-and-now.

23

*What was before and what is now
as suchness is the same intrinsical vastness;
such is the buddha-process
and suchness is its nature.*

The Perfection of the Process:
The past is known only through the thought constructs of memory, which are the reality of pure mind. The present is the field of reality that is known by pristine awareness. The future, like the past, is known only as mental constructs or projections, which, again, are the reality of pure mind. The actuality, the thing-in-itself, the suchness of past, present and future is an identical vast and spacious gnosis. The buddha-modality through which the past is known does not differ from the modality by which the future is known and neither differ from the present modality which is unstructured reality itself. Past, present and future are all known in the here-and-now and the buddha-modality through which they are understood is identical.

So the here-and-now is the whole process
like the moon and its reflection at one;
yet being total sameness,
it cannot be seen with a selective focus.

An Image of the Process:
The universal process, all-inclusive, is buddha's reality. It embraces everyone, knowing and unknowing, and all experience, because the process itself is reality. Reality is like the moon in the sky and its reflection in water made one; like the identity of the moon and the finger pointing at the moon; like the identity of the moon and its verbal indicator. The ultimate sameness of buddha and sentient beings is the pure pleasure reality that is invisible insofar as it is unobjectified. Focusing upon a single object of the senses as if it were a concrete entity, in a fixed, directed, gaze, partial in that it is selective, this ultimate sameness remains elusive.

Thus the nature of the reality-process is shown. The previous verse first does so from the point of view of buddha past, present and future, whose experience of it is identical; while this verse describes its nature as all-inclusive, embracing both buddha and all living creatures.

The Timeless Moment of Desirelessness

25

Present pleasure and future pleasure,
are direct perception and its shadow:
such calculation is a mistake—
do not trust it.

Unpredictable Pristine Awareness:
To believe that a moment of transcendent happiness will automatically lead to another because the present moment of direct perception is the 'front side' of pristine awareness whereas the next moment is its 'backside' is an error. To attribute 'front' and 'back', 'anterior' and 'posterior', or any relational attribution to pristine awareness is a glitch in the process. To calculate any aspect of pure mind's pristine awareness is to invite disaster, as calculation implies dependence upon fictional constructs such as past and future.

The notion of a 'shadow' of direct perception is derived from attachment to its pure pleasure and hope for repeated pleasure. Attachment to the memory of bliss can generate delusive supportive constructs, like 'past' and 'future', which undermine the awareness in which bliss is naturally inherent. Pristine awareness transcends all such attachment and it is equivocal therefore in that it defies prediction.

Thus the detachment, or desirelessness, in pristine awareness is demonstrated.

The Timeless Moment of Primordial Vastness

26

Past, present and future are one, without distinction,
the past never arisen, the future never arising;
embraced by pure being all is one,
immanent as an exalted vastness.

The Unequivocal Unity of Time:
In the mind of buddha there is only the here-and-now. In their pristine awareness there has never been any past and there never will be any future. The unity of here and now precludes the possibility of time. It is only the mental habits of human beings that create discrete past, present and future. Within pure being's unity of time, in the pristine awareness of exalted reality, is spontaneous pure pleasure. Without unity of time, the pure pleasure of immanent reality is not present.

Thus the primordial timelessness of the exalted essence of pure mind is disclosed (see verse 24).

The Timeless Moment of Freedom from Aspiration and Ambition

27

With full involvement in the threefold universe
ideas appear as delusory enchantment;
even the capital of the universal emperor
is a place conditioned by illusion.

The Utter Perfection of the Mundane World:
Fully engaged in the world, we are motivated by happiness and profit, fame and reputation, committed to the pleasures of the

senses, aesthetic appreciation and perhaps to high ideals. Here, phenomena are ultimately uncreated and uncaused, but they appear in a relative universe where ideas determine their illusory form and experience is known through verbal constructs. The whole is a web of delusory enchantment (*maya*). Insofar as that engagement is a purifying process, the merit accumulated in the relative world may lead to a seat of power, or even to the throne of the universal emperor. But that, also, is illusion.

The natural perfection of the threefold universe, the sky, the earth and the underworld, is a given, even when there is active and committed engagement therein and regardless of the eminence and power-status achieved by accumulation of merit. Pure mind is inescapable. Further, all mundane aspirations and desires, regardless of their fulfilment, are subsumed by pure mind and nothing can escape it. But the illusions of power—physical, economic, military, political, spiritual—have no credibility and maya, illusion, is the one cause for humor.

Thus complete perfection regardless of action or intent is asserted.

28

Those whose lives are slaves of time
never see an outcome in the moment;
if activity is fraught with hope
it can only be 'empty' action.[29]

The Utter Perfection of Mundane Motivation:
If we conduct our lives on a strict schedule, believing in the future, setting goals now for later attainment, no goal can arise in the present. Insofar as the present is continuously prostituted to the future no goal can ever be achieved in the present. Serving time means never seeing a goal achieved in the moment. Yet our daily round, our schedule of events, is dependant upon a fictional

construct of the future which in nature is an absence, and thus the here-and-now is always with us. Even though our daily agendas are fraught with desire, motivated by ambition, our goals located in a nonexistent future unattainable, even as we try to reify emptiness as a concrete achievement, our activity remains forever empty. In exertion motivated by desire, emptiness lies in the absence of a result or a product. Knowing emptiness as an absence, rather than as an inherent quality, actuates the perfection of the moment—appearances and existence are empty of everything else, not empty in themselves.

This verse shows that the inherent perfection of the moment can be actuated even when the discursive planning mind is forever running into a nonexistent future. It indicates that past, present and future, and mental constructs relating particularly to the future, are inescapably embraced by pure mind.

Thus, even though our desires create a counter-productive dependence on time, and we hold concrete notions of past and future, there is, nevertheless, automatic access to pure mind.

The Timeless Moment of Transmission Revealed

29

Utterly free of image, as one,
the yogin is like the imprint of a bird in the sky;
in the unstructured, unborn essence
where are the vaunted signs of his passing?

The Revelation of All Things As One—The Root of All Experience:
The nature of mind and pure mind is one, completely free of any form and, particularly, free of any temporal attribute—an

incalculable singularity. The yogin knows the nature of mind quite beyond its fabrications and fictions, and his gnosis is like an imprint of a bird in the sky and his mastery of the flow like the flight-path of a bird and his reality is like unthinking space. The pure essence of mind is as empty and unstructured as the imprint of a bird in the sky since it has no cause and is free of all conditions. Everything whatsoever occurs in pure essence of mind. Yet nothing whatsoever is substantial there and nor is there any evidence of something or nothing. Nothing arises from any cause; nothing is created by any condition; so from the beginning pure mind is free of all biased judgement imputing reality here and delusion there, truth here and a lie there, significance here and futility there, inflating this meaning and deflating that. The yogin leaves no trace of his achievement or the manner by which it was accomplished, no doctrine or dogma, no signs or indications. Here, the transmission is the one nature of mind—all of the buddha's teaching is the one nature of mind.

Every moment and every experience is the inspired revelation of Samantabhadra. No revelation has any greater significance than any other. Everything is transmission and there is no specific 'dharma path', just the all-inclusive modality. The image of the yogin as the flight-path of a bird may be considered a *koan*, the inconceivable construct that silences the mind and identifies it with infinite space, and this may constitute a transmission of the singularity of pure mind.

Thus there is transmission of nonspecific unity.

30

Inner and outer are one, the inner the outer itself,
so there are no hidden depths to discover;
under the power of the fictive world
samadhi lacks ultimate equality.

Nondifferentiation of Inner and Outer:
The chalice and the elixir, the vessel and the content, body and mind and so on, are inseparable, the one a mere proposition of the other. Therefore no hidden or 'inner' dimension exists to be known. Exoteric and esoteric are indivisible. Everything is upfront and in our faces. If we are bewitched by the verbal designations of mental fabrication and we labor under the delusion that there is an esoteric 'inner' reality to discover, then the essential quality of sameness will remain elusive. Belief in the dichotomy of inner and outer locks the yogin in a conceptual trap. Conversely, the samadhi that realizes the identity of inner and outer, because neither inner nor outer actually exist, recognizes universal equality in pure mind.

In pure mind our inner and outer lives are one because the outer itself is the inner and the inner the nature of the outer and there nothing is hidden or covert. What has significance is the here-and-now—which is totally complete in itself. This identification of outer and inner applies also to public and private lives. Complete transparency and invisibility are par for the course.

Thus transmission has no dimension and what you see is what you get.

31

And again about 'outer' and 'inner',
the body-mind is undifferentiated space;
and past, present and future inseparable within it,
all such designations are redundant.

Spatial and Temporal Unity:
In the samadhi that is utterly free of mental constructs, 'outer' and 'inner' cannot be computed. They cannot be identified and no distinction can be made between them. They cannot be

differentiated. Thus if the psycho-organism, the body-mind, composed of the five aggregates (name and form, feeling, perception, volition and consciousness) is what is referred to by 'outer', as an indeterminable and incalculable reality it is only present as the 'inner' indeterminable element of space. If 'inner' refers to the sense fields (the sense organs and their objects and the consciousness of each), again, outer and inner are inseparable as nothing is there but undifferentiated space. Further, through time indefinable reality cannot be separated from its spaciousness. So it is specious to say, 'This is the inner,' and 'That is the outer.' No such designation can be made.

In the vajrayana, the samayas and commitments are divided into inner and outer sections. We pledge to sustain awareness of the aggregates of the psycho-organism (name and form, sensation, perception, volition and consciousness) as buddhas and the components of the sense fields as bodhisattvas. Since no distinction can be made between the outer aggregates and inner space, or the outer senses and inner space, and since there is no distinction between past, present and future, spatial and temporal unity obtains and even the word 'commitment' is redundant.[30]

Thus the transmission has spatial and temporal unity.

The Timeless Moment of Sameness

32

The immovable is the seal of pure being,
the imperturbable is pristine awareness;
appropriating nothing, there is no self,
rejecting nothing, unutterable sameness.

The Complete Perfection of Being and Awareness:
Pure mind never becomes any thing, never becomes any shape, size, or color. Therefore insofar as it never moves out of its own nature it is immovable and unchangeable, and as such it is called the seal of pure being, which is free of perceptual duality. The self-sprung awareness of pure being remains constant in an imperturbable samadhi. In nondual perception nothing is appropriated from reality because there is no thing to take and no self to do the grasping and capturing. Refusing nothing, rejecting nothing, everything that arises in the mind fully accepted without discrimination, there is no repression. Through immovability, imperturbability and nondiscrimination, we can say 'Unutterable, nonverbal, sameness!'

The Immovable is ultimate, immutable sameness of all experience in terms of pure being or the inherent absence of structure to reality, and the Imperturbable is the pristine awareness of pure being. The former is the mudra or consort of the latter in a primordial and timeless union. In another context Immovable pure mind is represented as Achala (Miyowa) and imperturbable samadhi is Akshobhya (Mikyopa). This union of pure being and pristine awareness is also treated in verses 6 and 20.

33

The what, who and where,
our psychic modes and behavior, occur in pure mind;
but of any distinction between man and woman
the Lord of Sameness has nothing to say.

Exaltation of Enlightened Identity:
The seeming specifics of our lives, who and what we are, our mental environments and psychological states, our dominant passions, the karmic drives that determine our behavior, the various forms of acting out as gods, titans, hungry ghosts, animals

and devils—all this is pure mind itself and pure essence of mind. Samantabhadra, the personification of the pure essence of mind, makes no mention in the Dzogchen tantras of any distinction between man and woman in his all-inclusive space of sameness and implies, therefore, no gender distinction in the pure mind modality.

Thus the sameness of character, that of personality and that of gender are the ultimate equality of pure mind.

The Timeless Moment of Detachment from Bliss

34

Renunciation and fierce asceticism
provide no definitive answer;
but endowed with the A and the PA,[31]
the pleasure of delusory enchantment is assured.

The Immanent Perfection of Renunciation:
In the reality where there is nothing to find, if we seek to discipline the six senses through monastic privation or self-mutilating asceticism, no certain result can be achieved and no place to settle can be found. In this state of indeterminacy, however, the Disciples (*shravakas*), the auditors, who elude suffering through renunciation, may experience the fleeting pleasure of delusory enchantment. In the terms of atiyoga (which are not accepted by the Disciples) when endowed with the glyph A, which represents the conduit of the transmission and provides access to the level of the teacher, the glyph PA which represents the illusory emanation that provides the pleasure is also present.

This ambiguous verse thus serves to demonstrate the perfection immanent in the Disciples' renunciant method whereby the glyphs

A and PA may be the occasion for pure pleasure while receiving instruction. On the surface, however, it appears to treat tantra-yoga. Practice of relentless asceticism, providing an equivocal, indeterminate space, allows the bliss of *mahasiddhi* to arise in the yoga of union. Attachment to this bliss is pre-empted, however, by the intrinsic union of the glyphs A and PA, representing pure mind as coincident source and manifestation (see verse 19).

Thus attachment to the bliss is avoided.

35

Due to the indeterminacy of oneness,
however it is perceived so it appears:
the pleasure coveted in appearances,[32]
that is a heavy obscuring veil.

The Equivocal Nature of Experience:
In the mahayana sutras, it is said that phenomenal appearances are like the reflection of the moon in water. They are optical illusion, mirage, dream, echo, fairy castles in the sky, hallucination, rainbow, lightning, water bubbles, and a reflection in a mirror. Through appropriate contemplation, phenomena indeed appear like that. Thus, the perceiver's gaze conditioned by karmic proclivities determines the form of experience. In this way indeterminate pure mind appears as it is perceived, or appears in whatever way it is conditioned.

Striving to positively determine the nature of appearances that are infinitely variable obviates the pleasure in the nature of mind. When pleasure is the quality that is sought after in indeterminate experience—which is usually the case—the pleasure that is a projection imposed by mental habit, the striving for it obscures the pleasure innate in all appearances. To covet and hanker after pleasure is self-defeating. In nondual perception there is no object to focus upon, but when mental habit defines a part of that totality as a potential source of pleasure it is objectified and the pleasure in the *mahasiddhi* of nondual realization vanishes. Obsession with an externalized mental projection is an egregious glitch in the Dzogchen process.

Attachment to a seemingly existent quality 'out there' is implicit in desire for a sexual object. Accepting the nonexistent nature of all phenomena and experience, and understanding them to be the insubstantial though seemingly concrete projections of our mental habits, that attachment is broken.

Thus we are warned against projecting appearances that merely serve to satisfy desire.

36

The method of tantric pure mind practice
requires visualization of divine attire
as the moon's reflection in water;
nakedness and detachment emerge—
but this meditation is like the play of a child.

The Reality of Tantra-yoga:
The technique employed in the innumerable methods of outer yogatantra (tantra-yoga) is visualization of symbolic forms. In this practice, with the intellect, a buddha-deity is visualized along with his color, symbolic tokens and mudras, and in a mental trance the pellucid though illusory vision appears. Then the buddha-deity as a being of pristine awareness (*jnana-sattva*), stripped of all dualistic marks and signs and detached from any sense of self, unites with the desireless yogi. But this outer yogatantra meditation is like building sand-castles, an infantile, self-defeating preoccupation. Pristine awareness is realized with desirelessness,

but it is dependant upon an intellectual exercise that must be repeated again and again as the vision repeatedly collapses.

Thus it is evident that the practice of yogatantra may induce the bliss of *mahasiddhi*, but the bliss is a function of technique and therefore fleeting.

37

Identifying with the body of Mahakrodha
in his mandala of wrathful attributes,
even if the seed-syllable is actualized
nirvana itself cannot be seen.

The Reality of Creative Mahayoga:
In mahayoga meditation, the mandala of consciousness is visualized with the visionary attributes of divine wrath with the wrathful deity Mahakrodha at the center. After repetitive practice, identifying with the visualized body of Mahakrodha, the deity actually manifests. Then the seed syllable HUNG, matured by habit, may emerge, and thereby the wide open, uncontrived nature which is ultimate peace and serenity is discovered. This is not the same thing, however, as perceiving nirvana through direct sensory perception. Mahayoga brings the yogin to the point of nirvana only within his formal samadhi.

In this verse the bliss of *mahasiddhi* is realized through mahayoga mandala visualization and the actualization of the syllable HUNG. In the Great Perfection, attachment is pre-empted by understanding of the limited nature of this siddhi.

Thus mahayoga is a contrived meditation technique that leads the way to Dzogchen Ati.

38

*Under the sway of emotion,
by lopping the top off the palm tree,
or incinerating the seed,
the tyranny of emotion is avoided:
so it is taught.*

Undiminishing, Inviolable Perfection:
The discipline and vows of the Disciples (*shravakas*), Hermits (*pratyekabuddhas*), and Sutra Bodhisattvas deteriorate under the influence of emotion. Their way of dealing with passion, suppression and sublimation ('cutting the top off the palm tree'), or applying an appropriate antidote, is thus thwarted and there is no advantage. In the vajrayana, the homeopathic method of eradicating the root cause of passion ('incinerating the seed') is futile if the samaya commitments are not maintained. On the contrary, because the Dzogchen samaya commitment is unformed and therefore unbreakable it provides immunity to all external and internal conditions.

It is folly to attempt to destroy attachment and the foundation of emotion when under the sway of passion. In the graduated process of eradicating emotion, passion is still present to undermine the commitments that are the sole protection against backsliding. The Dzogchen samaya-commitment that is no samaya, the spontaneous perfection of the moment, guarantees that it can never deteriorate or degenerate.

Thus attachment to the bliss of the *mahasiddhi* arising within the practice of the yoga of union on the tantric path is shown to be avoided through the Dzogchen samayas.

39

Each of the hundreds and thousands of techniques
bears an appropriate flower:
unmarked signless perfection
has no particular abode.

The Perfecting Nature of Mind—the Perfection of All Paths: Where there is a technique, a causal process and a practice, there is a goal, a product and an effect. Though the goal be even so subtle a state of mind as bliss, if it can be found it can also be lost. But since all methods and all goals arise within the pure mind that is complete perfection they cannot but partake of the nature of purity. Dzogchen, however, is an unmarked path, and there is no sign of attainment—not even a small flower. Conversely, due to the signlessness of Dzogchen reality which is emptiness, the abodes of the pleasure-seeking world cannot emerge under its power and the heavenly abodes, or trance states, created by meditation techniques cannot appear. Still, the myriad techniques of tantra and the lower approaches continue to be embraced by the pure and perfect nature of mind.

Thus the signlessness of the Dzogchen modality precludes emergence of attachment to the pleasure of union and desire for mundane happiness.

The Timeless Moment of Effortlessness

40

Present here with a silent mind
the yogin is fortunate indeed;
self and other indistinguishable,
he revels in the arena of enchanted spontaneity.

Evidence of Enlightenment:
The yogin's mind is silent insofar as all the evaluative and judgmental discussion within himself is transcended in the pure mind reality. He knows the unstructured, unfabricated, nature of it, and his activity and his compassionate mind come together. In this lies his great fortune. For nothing has caused his pleasure which is totally adventitious. With a silent mind, in the pure potential of space, he has nothing to do for himself and with nothing to urge him to act he has nothing to do for others. His reality is an enchanted illusion, spontaneously, effortlessly, occurring, and there he plays in a natural field of reality. In a state of blissful enchantment the yogin embodies the exaltation of buddhahood here and now.

Thus an image of effortless, undirected action is presented affirming the natural authenticity of buddhahood.

The Timeless Moment of Unchanging Reality

41

Totally complete, all-inclusive,
unchanging, it is simply being;
and like unbounded space,
reality is contingent upon nothing.

The Sublime Teaching—The Great Perfection:
Samantabhadra is the constant and universal teacher and pure mind is the timeless teaching. Everything that is revealed is disclosed by Samantabhadra; what is disclosed is always pure mind. Pure mind is the great perfection, the essence of all experience, and everything is always all-inclusive, nothing wanting, complete and perfect in itself. Nothing need ever be done—indeed nothing can be done—to improve or alter

experience. It is self-sufficient, so it can never be dependent upon anything or anyone else. It is immutable and unchangeable, so no progress is possible. It is always up-front and in our faces, so there is nothing hidden to be disclosed. Complete and perfect, it is without cause or effect, so nothing is dependant upon anything else.

Thus we are provided a celebration of the great perfection.

42

*Pure pleasure arises spontaneously
from the intrinsic power of gnosis,
and solely and exclusively as pristine awareness;
reality cannot be anywhere else.*[33]

The Reality of Dzogchen Atiyoga:
Gnosis is self-cognition, the yoga of Dzogchen Ati. Freedom from causality and conditioning is the environment in which spontaneity occurs: naturally potent, self-sprung awareness. The nature of pristine awareness is incommensurate with any seemingly concrete name and form, and is inimical to it. Thus experience, which is pure pleasure, occurs only in spontaneous gnosis.

Pure pleasure is the magical radiance in gnosis of pure mind's pristine awareness. Its spontaneity indicates an absence of all causal and conditional factors. Pure mind is all-inclusive and utterly autonomous, and its pristine awareness, naturally self-sprung, transcends every causal process and immediately dissolves any delusory name and form. Timeless spontaneity is the seal of Dzogchen Ati.

Thus the timeless blissful spontaneity of primal gnostic awareness is the reality of Dzogchen Ati and is intrinsic to all experience which can be nothing other than pure pleasure.

43

Easy and difficult, difficult because so easy,[34]
pure mind, invisible, is all-pervasive;
it cannot be pointed out by name—
even Vajrasattva cannot show it.

Unequivocal Absence of Any Indication of Attainment:
In the sense that pure mind has no cause or condition and is timelessly, spontaneously present, it is unavoidable and inevitable and therefore easy of access. But since there is no trace of its presence, never an object of focus, never a finite quality, it is impossible to conceptualize and therefore impossible to access. There is no word or definition big enough to identify it because it embraces the entire phenomenal world. Even Vajrasattva himself cannot particularize it or pin it down. For this reason, no degree of facility in it can be evaluated.

Thus since pure mind is inseparable from direct perception it cannot be accessed and yet nor can it be evaded.

The Timeless Moment Uncaused and Unconditioned

44

This marvelous, miraculous display,
undirected, freeform, like space,
out of amorphous bewilderment
it arises momentarily, spontaneously.

The Perfection of Self-sprung Display:
This marvelous uncaused pure mind with its miraculous self-sprung unconditioned pristine awareness is a continuous, enjoyable phantasmagoria. Like space, this display is pure potential, requiring no effort or input or cultivation whatsoever.

Even within our bewilderment pristine awareness emerges instantaneously and adventitiously. The stupor of bewilderment lacking sustained focus or image or concrete idea facilitates pristine awareness because it cannot be crystalized, confined or obstructed. Bewilderment is thus the basis of the uncaused miracle of momentary display of unimaged illusion. The light ocean of awareness is not the flip side of the dark ocean—it is the dark ocean itself.

Thus even stupidity is suffused by pure mind (see also *Pure Golden Ore* verse 5).

45

This is the all-inclusive modality
naturally present in all beings;
in the dust-storm of blighting delusion
we call for medicine though mind's nature is the cure.[35]

The Equivocating, Doubting Intellect:
The notion that all beings, whatever their intelligence, moral status or state of mind, are included on the path of pure mind, is difficult for the intellect to swallow. Habituated to the distinctions of high and low, pure and impure, intelligent and stupid, and to the idea of a graduated, structured path upon which progress is determined by karma, it is difficult to assimilate the immanence of reality. Even though the rational mind is included in the nondual pure mind modality, the immature intellect left insecure, continues to doubt. Without gnosis we are tainted by delusion and search for an extraneous cure, although the master of medicine is our own mind. We know that buddha is the mind itself, but regardless we continue to look for the solution outside, constantly shifting our focus of search when, inevitably, we fail to find it.

This verse shows that even the slightest motivation to seek the great perfection precludes finding it.

The Timeless Moment of Universal Enlightenment

46

In the field of ordinary experience lies pure pleasure,
itself the pristine purity of mundane existence;
in every perception finite light is concentrated
and boundless space is established.

The Sublime Retinue:
We all know that the nature of mind is buddha and that in the field of gnosis buddha is pure pleasure. This understanding accesses the open dimension of mundane existence.[36] There is no particular object to focus upon. Indeed, focus, or reification, precludes access to the pure pleasure. Relaxation into any and all random sensory experience opens up the innate purity of our ordinary world, an experience concentrated in heightened awareness and known as light. Our sense organs naturally concentrate the light of experience while consciousness extends it filling the ten directions of space (the cardinal and intermediate directions, the zenith and nadir)—which is boundless space—and illuminating it (see verse 50). Through this simultaneous process of concentration and radiation, all phenomena are experienced as buddha-deity and pure mind. Such is the instantaneous process of enlightenment.

The concentration and radiation of light in the sense organs parallels the absorption and emergence of light by Samantabhadra in the field of reality. Whatever he radiates and absorbs is his perfect retinue. His retinue in pure being (dharmakaya) consists of all buddha past, present and future and all sentient beings of the sensual, aesthetic and formless realms and of the six streams of consciousness. His retinue in the mode of enjoyment (sambhogakaya) comprises all fleeting emotion and knowledge. His retinue in the emanation mode (nirmanakaya, tulku) are the appearances of compassion that are the six kinds of being, the conditioned mind and the ocean of activities. His relationship to the retinue, though a unity, is the same as the relationship of space to the other four great elements; the relationship of Dzogchen as perfect reality to the 84,000 techniques of the pure mind process; and the relationship of pure essence of mind to the sensory process.

The concentration of light through awareness may appear to reveal a method, a yoga of approach, a door into Vajrasattva's reality, and thus constitute a contrived technique; but the process of absorption of light in the sensory focus and the simultaneous radiation of the light of consciousness into boundless space is innate, and need not be vouchsafed.

This verse and the next show how buddhahood is revealed in the moment to everyone.

47

Out of nebulous rainbow light
the families' distinctive qualities appear;
likewise, as vibrating particles unmoving,
the Lord rules the five elements.

The Consummation of Ubhaya-yoga:
In nebulous, amorphous oneness there can be no differentiation of the five families' five distinct colors and qualities. Yet the rainbow light of oneness, like a beam of white light diffracted into a spectrum, is variegated in the mind as five separate colors—white, blue, red, yellow and green. Within those colors the five buddha-families appear with their specific qualities of consciousness.

Likewise, without moving one iota the nature of mind becomes visible in all-inclusive self-sprung awareness. This is Vajrasattva, the overlord of the five elements, and the five elements are the five buddhas.

Ubhaya, or charya yoga, partakes of both the macrocosmic qualities of kriya-yoga and the mental elements of yogatantra. Here the enigma of unity and multiplicity identical is resolved in the reality of Vajrasattva. In this ubhaya-yoga vision, Vajrasattva is, simultaneously, unitary rainbow light and the efflorescence of the variegated fivefold colors of the five buddha-families out of which the sensory fields manifest. Likewise, he is both the unmoving field out of which the five great vibrating elements arise and the elements themselves that compose the illusory universe. At the center of this mandala of the buddha-families Vajrasattva is the unitary reality (see also verse 4).

Thus all beings are already enlightened by Vajrasattva's all-penetrating reality.

The Timeless Moment of Ganachakrapuja

48

'Past', 'present' and 'future',
these labels are redundant;
to comprehend what is unborn and unceasing
is to know the sublime unity of time.

Pith Instruction on Notional Time:
'Past', 'present' and 'future' are nominal abstractions. 'The past' and 'the future' can never exist in the here-and-now and 'the present' exists only as a relational concept. To conceive of past and future is a glitch in the Dzogchen perspective. Past, present and future never come into existence and never pass into

nonexistence: what we have in reality is the sublime unity of time, timelessness, or Great Time. To conceive of and comprehend the three times as uncreated and unceasing is secret instruction on the unity of past, present and future.

Every moment is a great feast celebration. It is a spontaneous function of the sublime unity of time and space. There is no possibility of temporal structure in pure mind reality. Comprehending the unity of time, each moment is complete and perfect in itself. The basis of ritual procedure is thereby undermined, destroying any and all attachment to the process.

The great feast offering (*ganachakrapuja*; Tibetan: *tsok-cho*) is the central tantric celebration of the nature of reality through sensory indulgence. It is usually performed as a congregational rite. Verses 48 to 54 relate to aspects of the Dzogchen vision as the great feast offering.

This verse and the next establish the redundancy of ritual, along with past, present and future, as fictional mental constructs (see also verse 26).

49

In sameness there can be no temporal construct,
in oneness no projection or dedication;
the adorning offerings, naturally arranged,
through their intrinsic perfection, defy preparation.

Unequivocal Identity of the Guru and the Offering:
Past and future are identical, so the stages of preparation and enactment of offering are the undifferentiated here and now. Through the logic of experiential singularity, the offering, which comprises all phenomena whatsoever, pristine awareness and the yogin who offers up all phenomena, these three, are identical. In this unitary reality, there is no trace of anything concrete

anywhere, no reification of offerings, and no distinction between the yogin and the offering. Since there is no dualistic projection, there is nothing to be ritually dedicated. The offerings, adornments of the field of reality, are the five sensual pleasures (sight, sound, taste, smell and touch) that arise spontaneously in an arbitrary yet perfect arrangement in natural timeless gnosis. The absence of any arrangement is itself the perfect arrangement.

Thus gnosis, the donor and the offering are one in spontaneous giving where dedication and arrangement are redundant.

50

Spontaneity precludes any dedication of offering—
naturally pure, the offering is already ambrosia;
the specific senses and consciousness,
in the highest samadhi, are indivisible.

Unequivocal Absence of Motivation in Offering:
The offering is always the ornamented field of reality, the totality of the moment. This vast all-inclusive offering is timelessly and spontaneously present and in its very presence is made as an offering. Spontaneity precludes the fiction of 'dedication' which implies a reification or conceptualization of offering and a projective transference. Besides, the intrinsic perfection of the offering preempts the need for any dedication. If there is a dualistic perception of the yogin making the offering and the offering itself then notwithstanding since that dichotomy is naturally resolved from the very beginning the offering is already ambrosia. In the yogin's highest samadhi the concentrating power of the six senses and the proliferating function of the six consciousness (see verse 46) are a unity and in that perceptual nonduality the blessing is achieved. Any visualization is redundant.

Thus offering is a natural spontaneous function in the here-and-now.

The Timeless Moment of Spontaneously Perfected Offering of Sensual Pleasure.

51

The projecting intellect is the giver,
in the power of the gaze lies the natural arrangement;
the siddhi inherent in clear seeing,
that is perfect meditative equipoise.

Making the Universal Offering Through the Intellect:
In the subtle ritual function of offering, the intellect is the giver, dedicating all phenomena as the offering through a subtle projection of giving into boundless space. A natural asymmetrical arrangement of the five sensual pleasures (sight, sound, smell, taste and sensation) is implicit in the sensory gaze.[37] Perceiving the offering as sensorialy imaged, in the clarity or luminosity of the five sensual pleasures lies the siddhi (or realization). In the siddhi resides the samadhi of meditative equipoise. Therein, the accumulation of merit as a causal basis of wish-fulfilment and pristine awareness itself are immediately completed.

Thus both the natural function of offering in the moment and the intrinsical spontaneous perfection of ritual offering are described.

The Timeless Moment of Spontaneity

52

A flash of apprehension is union,
blissful satisfaction is the commitment;

moving in the dance of skillful means,
nondual union is the offering.

Pith Instruction in Nonunion:
Each moment of experience as the nature of mind is a consummate transcendent union. Therein adventitious bliss is the formless commitment (samaya) that is naturally sustained. Within the gnosis of that moment, the field of empty wisdom is momentarily revealed; in the dance of transforming illusion, whatever seeming situations and positions arise are an offering in the wholeness of pure mind identity. The tantric components of 'union', 'commitment', 'skillful means' and 'offering' are defined in terms of nonduality.

In the great perfection of the nature of mind there is no temporal process wherein two become one because from the beginning there has never been any separation. All is one in pure mind. So 'union' is a recognition of the inexpressible nature of pure mind, wherein pure pleasure is always the feeling tone. Although in anuyuga pure mind is defined in terms of the union of gnosis and the field of reality,[38] still that union is never consummated and never cloven and the skillful dance is a constant offering.

Thus the great feast rite is momentary spontaneity.

The Timeless Moment of Infinite Ritual

53

Detached generosity is the torma
and nonaction instantaneously completes the ritual;
unthought pristine awareness dissolves obstacles,
and unspoken meditative equipoise is the hymn of praise.

The Consummation of Ritual Performance:
Each moment is a spontaneous non-ritual *torma* offering. In gnosis the phenomenal world is utterly forsaken without a shred of grasping, clinging—or even apprehension. In the space of complete equality no action is superior to any other. But when the ritual of torma offering, for example, is performed, perceptual nonduality is represented by the torma—a cone-shaped parched barley cake laced with molasses decorated with symbols of transcendence to represent aspects of buddha-mind. Non-directed action transcends the yogin's performance of the ritual, which is, therefore, consummated before it is done. Here unthinking pristine awareness is the Lord of the Directions; here the Lord of Obstructing Forces immediately dissolves the subtle obstacles and thought-forms, personified as *gek*s, drawn to the offering ritual; and here nonverbal meditative equipoise is the Lord of Uncontrived Activity, Lord of Nonaction, who sings the hymns of praise. In this way the elements of ritual naturally express the spontaneous moment to moment pure mind modality and the ritual performance of kriya-yoga—vajra-kriya—is perfected by the transcendent nature of mind.

The Timeless Moment of the Great Bind: The Chains of Self-important Giving

54

Veneration of the lama and generosity
and all such meritorious activity
enacted without imperturbable detachment
become a serious bind.

The Glitch of Goal-directed Action:
In the process of the great perfection, in the Dzogchen modality, it is not the nature of the action but the attitude that counts, and

bad attitude is disclosed in attachment to a goal or attention to the result of an action. Even if the result is the virtue that serves one's own or another's purpose, like moral conduct and patience, goal-orientation puts the mind into a dualistic frame and binds it. Worshiping the guru-lama with offerings given for the purpose of receiving blessing or some mundane benefit, or giving alms to beggars or gifts to friends with an ulterior motive, is a glitch in the pure mind process unless it is performed with the complete indifference provided by an immovable samadhi of desirelessness.

This glitch in behavior—which may by extension apply to any activity wherein attachment lies—is stressed as a terrible bind, not so much as through the self-involvement inherent in the act but through goal-directed motivation. Without the samadhi of equality we are caught in a double bind. We are wrong if we do not worship the teacher; we are wrong if we venerate him with regular attachment. We must make offering; but only without attachment. In the praxis of the great perfection, however, the great bind is reflexively-released. Come what may, the nature of the moment is spontaneously resolved.

Thus we gain release from lama-worship.

The Timeless Moment of Symbolic Transmission

55

About this very transmission,
if it is structured it becomes a veil;
if conceptualized, similarly
its reality can never be achieved.

Seminal Instruction on this Great Transmission:
If we search for meaning we are bound by it and lose it. If we strive for effortlessness we cannot find it. So in this transmission

of total perfection if effortless non-seeking turns into striving we are diseased and veiled. If, however, we realize nonaction here and now reality can never become concrete.

The purpose of this transmission is to resolve all experience whatsoever in complete perfection. Inasmuch as experience consists of comprehension of the meaning of the transmission its purpose is to deconstruct and dissolve the veils that hide its reality. So to structure its content in any way is to defy its purpose. To conceptualize its meaning or to turn it into a religious practice or a yoga is to defeat its objective. Ambiguity is an intrinsic element of its dynamic. Insofar as we seek solid meanings its internal dialectic is frustrated.

Thus we are cautioned that the words of the transmission are the finger pointing at the moon and not the moon itself.

Endnotes

NB. See Appendix I for abbreviations used in the notes.

1. See Patrul Rimpoche, "The Three Incisive Precepts", Dowman 2003, p. 181.
2. Vairotsana first received from Shri Singha the Eighteen Mind Series transmissions, including his own five early translations (*Snga 'gyur lnga*) and thirteen transmissions translated later by Vimalamitra, and then the Matrix Series transmissions.
3. This account of Vairotsana is derived from various, sometimes conflicting sources. The most significant variation is the location of Vairotsana's encounter with Shri Singha which is given as Vajrasana (Bodh Gaya) in some sources, most particularly in the *Bairo 'dra 'bag* (Yudra Nyingpo 2004), the standard hagiography of Vairotsana, where 'Vajrasana' may be understood figuratively as the seat of enlightenment. See also Namkhai Norbu and Adriano Clamente 1999, pp. 46-56.
4. The six lines of the *Cuckoo's Song (Rig pa'i khu byug)* are called *The Six Vajra Verses (Rdo rje tshig drug)* in the *Kun byed rgyal po* where they are said to define the nature of Samantabhadra himself as spontaneously complete and perfect nonaction. The *Mdo bcu* commentary takes the verses to be a transmission of the precept of undiscriminating enjoyment.
5. The *Kun rje rgyal po* introduces *Radical Creativity (Rtsal chen sprugs pa)* like this: This great transmission is Samantabhadra's inspired precept and reveals the freeform immaculate reality-field as the field of his radical creativity, which is nonaction.
6. *The Great Garuda in Flight (Khyung chen lding ba)* should not be confused with Shri Singha's work or any of several others with similar titles. The *Mdo bcu* commentary distinguishes between a first part (vs. 1-16) that constitutes specific instruction, primarily on nonmeditation, and a second part (vs. 17- 26) that treats various aspects of the yogin's career.

Endnotes

7. In the *Gnas lugs mdzod 'grel ba*, p.84, f. 35, Longchenpa quotes this verse as: *Sems nyid rang snang gi rnam pa las/ stong pa 'gyur ba med pa'i dbyings shes bar byas.*
8. The 'nucleus' (*rdul phran gcig*) is at once an atomic particle that cannot be divided and the seminal seed of totality (*thig le nyag cig*). There are variant readings for *gses shing*.
9. 'Sacred and profane' renders 'dharma and nondharma' (*chos dang chos min*).
10. 'Sages' (*drang srong*) can refer to Indian rishis or to Bon monks.
11. See Namkhai Norbu and Adriano Clemente 1999, p.280, note 205 for Longchenpa's commentary on these first eleven verses.
12. This ambiguous line may also be read as 'all are free from conventional morality' or 'all have abandoned worldly sin' (*kha na ma tho 'jig rten spong*). See Longchenpa 2006, canto 122ii, p. 268.
13. See also *Pure Golden Ore* v. 8. The following seven lines have been removed from the body of translation because they seem to be an irrelevant interpolation breaking the flow of meaning (the *Mdo bcu* has no commentary on these lines). Perhaps they were added due to the strong force of their argument urging non-action, which is the topic of this transmission. *Because all experience is in the present / the nature of experience is the here-and-now; / so the phenomenal mind seeking itself, space seeking the nature of space / as if reality were something extraneous, / is like trying to extinguish fire with fire, / and that is a very difficult task.* The intellect cannot see or isolate its own nature and in the effort and striving to objectify itself it creates a stream of discursive analytic thought together with misguided ideas about how to achieve consummation that merely muddy the water further. Conversely trying to stop thinking merely creates further thought and is like adding fire to fire.
14. The title *Pure Golden Ore* (*Rdo la gser zhun*) provides a metaphor for the intrinsic purity of our every experience. Suffused by gold, ore is no less precious then purified gold itself. The Gentle Youth, who personifies the pure mind that suffuses all experience, is Manjushri Kumara ('Jam dpal gzhon nu), known more conventionally as the bodhisattva of intelligence and the protector of mind. Confounded with the pure essence of mind, the fount of all and everything, he is omniscient.
15. The text has *lo rgyus don gnyis* which may be taken to indicate both its absolute (*rang don*) and specific (*spyi don*) meaning. The *Mdo bcu* treats history (*lo rgyus*) under three headings: blessing (*byin brlabs*),

'own essence' (*rang gi ngo bo*), and scripture (*tshig sdebs*). The three samadhis are taken as *de bzhin nyid kyi ting nge 'dzin, kun tu snang gi ting nge 'dzin,* and *rgyu'i ting nge 'dzin.*

16. These twelve lines appended to *Pure Golden Ore* appear to be a later insertion. The *Mdo bcu* adds this concluding verse: *The all-transcending six nuclei / immune to any inflation or deflation / by dint of their unborn and unceasing nature / reveal the meaning of nonmeditation.* The six nuclei are: the nucleus of reality (*chos nyid kyi thig le*); the nucleus of the field of reality (*dbyings kyi thig le*); the nucleus of the field of utter purity (*dbyings rnam par dag pa'i thig le*); the nucleus of pristine awareness (*ye shes chen pa'i thig le*); the nucleus of Samantabhadra (*Kun tu bzang pa'i thig le*); and the nucleus of spontaneity (*lhun gyi grub pa'i thig le*). It may be relevant to note that some sources include the *Thig le drug pa* amongst the Five Early Translations.

17. Better known as *The Eternal Victory Banner* or *The Ever Unfurled Victory Banner (Mi nub rgyal mtshan), The Vast Space of Vajrasattva (Rdo rje sems dpa' nam mkha' che)* is introduced as the root of all pith instruction and transmission (BGB). In *Kun byed rgyal po* Samantabhadra introduces the transmission like this: *Listen, Sempa Dorje, / I will show you, Sempa Dorje, / your own nature. / I, the supreme source, I am your nature / and I am timeless pure mind / and pure mind is like this.*

18. The third sutra of the *Mdo bcu* treats the fivefold excellence of the teacher, the teaching, his retinue, the time and the place. The nature of the perfect teacher, Samantabhadra, is demonstrated here (v. 1); the excellent teaching is pure mind (v. 41 and also 42); the nature of the excellent retinue is the three modes of being within gnosis (v. 46); the excellent place is the vast field of reality (vs.16 and 9) ; the excellent time is the unity of time (vs. 26 and 48).

19. The fifth sutra of the *Mdo bcu* treats the five exaltations (*che ba rnam lnga*): The exaltation of enlightenment here and now (*mngon par sangs rgyas che*) expressed as the fivefold excellence (see note 18); exaltation of the enlightened field of reality (v. 16); exaltation of enlightened identity (v. 33); and exaltation of the evidence of enlightenment (v. 40).

20. The seventh sutra of the *Mdo bcu* treats the three kinds of transmission: Transmission ultimately resolving all experience (v. 3); direct transmission: emanation in the nature of mind (v. 19); and the aural transmission (v. 22).

Endnotes

21. Verses 4, 5 and 6 show the intrinsic perfection of the nature of mind, regardless of meditation technique. The *Mdo bcu* commentary upon these verses shows how mahayoga, anuyoga and sattva-yoga (vs. 4, 5 and 6 respectively), subsumed by Dzogchen, facilitate realization of this perfection.
22. TB has 'reality' (*chos nyid*); BGB has 'teaching' or 'dharma' (*chos 'di*).
23. The seventh sutra of the *Mdo bcu* treats pith instruction (*man ngag*, alternatively translated as 'secret precept'): On pure mind (v. 9), on nonunion (v. 52), on notional time (v. 48), and on seminal instruction on this great transmission (v. 55). See Longchenpa 2006, canto 84, p. 172, for the master's comment upon the status of karma presented in vs. 9 and 10.
24. The sixth sutra of the *Mdo bcu* treats glitches and veils in a sixfold enumeration: 1. The glitch of belief in progress on a path (v. 21); 2. the glitch of striving (v. 20); 3. the glitch of goal-directed action (v. 54); 4. the glitch of moral discrimination (v. 14); 5. the glitch of subtle method (v. 13); and 6. the glitch of concentrated absorption (v. 12).
25. Consider the *rdzogs rim* precepts of physical, verbal and mental solitude (*lus- sngags- sems- dben*).
26. The eighth sutra of the *Mdo bcu* treats the five certainties: 1. The unequivocal unity of time (v. 26); 2. unequivocal identity of the guru and the offering (v. 49); 3. unequivocal absence of motivation in offering (v. 50); 4. unequivocal absence of indication of attainment (v. 43); 5. unequivocal congruence of pleasure and pain (v. 15).
27. The fourth sutra of the *Mdo bcu* treats the four yogas: 1. The reality of Dzogchen atiyoga (v. 42); 2. the reality of Dzogchen anuyoga (v. 17); 3. the reality of creative mahayoga (v. 37); 4. the reality of tantra-yoga (v. 36). See *Great Garuda* v. 1 where the concept of the dharmakaya is equated with the dharmakaya itself and vs. 49 and 50 below where the reality of anuyoga is trumped by spontaneity.
28. Verses 18 and 19 treat reality in terms of language. A *dharani*, the *mudra*, is a formulation of gnosemes, a 'union' of vowels and consonants, that describes a seemingly concrete reality; yet as an emanation of dharmakaya it is empty buddha-speech. Joining with the *dharani* there is no distinction between the gnosemic or verbal formulation and the great display of Samantabhadra. But see v. 52 on Nonunion.
29. TB has *ma bral smon pas spyod pas na*; BGB *ma bral smon pa spyod pas na* and *Mdo bcu* supports this with *chags dang ma bral*. NCG has

bya bral smon pa spyod pas na and thus inverts the meaning: action unmotivated in time / this is 'empty action'; or, where conduct is unmotivated, that activity is said to be 'empty'.

30. The word *tha tshigs* in the first and last lines of the verse may be rendered as either a synonym of *tha snyad*, 'conventional designation', or as *dam tshig,* 'samaya', 'commitment'. The *Mdo bcu* takes the first interpretation.
31. BGB has: A *dang par ni rnam ldan na,* while the *Mdo bcu* has *Lung gi A dang ston pa'i sar ldan na.* See NCG chs. 7 and 8.
32. This line (*snang 'dod rtsol sems bde ba la* from TB is glossed in the *Mdo bcu* by 'hankering after appearances' (*snang bar 'dod cing rtsol sems byed pa*), which is the obscuration. See also *Great Garuda* v. 15 regarding this verse.
33. See Namkhai Norbu and Adriano Clemente 1999, p. 172, and Longchenpa 2006, canto 115, p. 216, which has a line interpolated between the 3rd and 4th lines: that is nondual knowledge and ignorance.
34. Rongzom (see Clemente 1999, p. 55, note 9) has 'contaminated' (*bslad*) instead of 'easy' (*sla*). The natural state is veiled by contaminating concepts. The phrase 'unequivocal absence of any indication of attainment' (*dka' sla mtshon du med pa*) that heads the commentary is an inadequate rendering of the notion that it is impossible to say whether access to pure mind is easy or difficult, or whether indeed there is any access at all.
35. BGB has: we innocents, because of tainting delusion / are like medicine seeking a doctor (*byis pas 'khrul pas bslad pa'i phyir / sman nyid sman pa 'tshol ba bzhin*). TB has: *bus pas bslad bas 'khrul pa'i phyir.*
36. On the progressive paths, understanding (*go ba*), experiencing (*nyams pa*), and realization (*rtogs pa*) are three stages of increasing assimilation of knowledge to the intellect. In this Dzogchen analysis, within mere comprehension (*go ba*), or within every fleeting thought or concept (*rtog pa*), lies realization (*rtogs pa*).
37. In the third line of the verse TB has 'the offering which is seen' (*bltas ba'i tshogs ni*) rather than BGB and *Mdo bcu* 'the power of the gaze' (*bltas ba'i stobs*).
38. In anuyoga the union of gnosis (*rig pa*) and the field of reality (*dbyings*) is represented by the union of father-buddha (Samantabhadra) and mother-buddha (Samantabhadri). On union see also vs. 5, 18 and 32.

Appendix I
The Tibetan Texts and Commentaries

The following abbreviations are used here and in the annotation:
BGB *Bairo rgyud 'bum*: 8 vols. Tashigangpa, Leh, 1971.
TB *Rnying ma rgyud 'bum, Mtshams brag* edition: 46 vols. Thimphu, Bhutan: National Library, Royal Government of Bhutan, 1982.
NCG *Rdo rje sems dpa' nam mkha' che'i rgyud*: (TB vol. Ga ff. 165.3-191.)

The Five Early Translations appear in the *Bairo rgyud 'bum* and as chapters of the *Kun byed rgyal po* (see below). They are also quoted in the *Mdo bcu* in the context of their commentary. The *Bairo rgyud 'bum* is the oldest but most corrupted. The commentary to the transmissions is derived primarily from the explanatory text the *Mdo bcu (Chos thams cad rdzogs pa chen po byang chub kyi sems su 'dus pa'i mdo)*: TB vol. Ka ff. 352-499, the second text in the *Rnying ma rgyud 'bum*. Of the various tantras in the *Rnying ma rgyud 'bum* with *Rdo rje sems dpa' nam mkha' che* in the title, the *Rdo rje sems dpa' nam mkha' che' i rgyud* has sometimes shed light on verses in the *Mi nub rgyal mtshan* and, likewise, the *Lcags 'grel* commentary (BGB vol. Nga pp. 397-453).

The following verses or lines are quoted by Longchenpa in *Byang chub kyi sems kun byed rgyal po'i don khrid rin chen sgru bo*, translated as *You Are the Eyes of the World* (Longchenpa 1987): *Radical Creativity* v. 6 on pp. 24-5; *Pure Golden Ore* v. 7 in note 42; *Eternal Victory Banner* v. 16 on p. 40; and v. 40 on p. 43.

The following verses or lines are quoted by Longchenpa in *Gnas lugs mdzod 'grel ba*, translated as *Old Man Basking in the Sun* (Longchenpa 2006): *Eternal Victory Banner* vs. 9 and 10 in canto 84, p. 172; v. 30 in canto 85, p. 174, and in canto 113, p. 213; and vs. 41, 42 and 44 in canto 115 p. 216. *Great Garuda* vs. 2-4 are quoted in canto 8 pp. 49-50; v. 10 in canto 33, p. 102; v. 12 in canto 63, p.141; v. 14 in canto 112, p. 212; and v. 21 in canto 125, p. 242.

APPENDICES

Sources of Tibetan Texts and English Translation

For the Nyingma collections of tantras see the Samantabhadra Collection online at the University of Virginia:
<http://www.thdl.org/collections/literature/nyingma.php>

Rig pa'i khu byug: The Cuckoo's Song of Gnosis
IOL/Stein 647 in the Tun Huang Collection.
TB vol. Ka 113.2-113.5; *Kun byed rgyal po*, ch. 31.
TB vol. Ka 453.3-453.6; *Mdo bcu*, in the eighth sutra.
BGB vol. Nga p.306.
Samten Karmay, 1988: p. 50.
John Reynolds, 1996: pp. 232-3.
Namkhai Norbu and John Shane, 1986: p. xv.
Namkhai Norbu and Adriano Clemente, 1989: p. 48.
Namkhai Norbu and Adriano Clemente, 1999: pp. 174.

Rtsal chen sprugs pa: Radical Creativity
TB vol. Ka ff. 98.7-100.1; *Kun byed rgyal po* ch. 27.
TB vol. Ka ff. 453.6-455.1; *Mdo bcu*, in the eighth sutra.
BGB vol. Nga pp. 306-308.
Namkhai Norbu and Adriano Clemente, 1999: p. 165.

Khyung chen lding ba: Great Garuda in Flight
TB vol. Ka ff. 87.2-91.6; *Kun byed rgyal po* ch. 22.
TB vol. Ka ff. 455.1-462.4; *Mdo bcu*, in the eighth sutra.
BGB vol Nga pp. 308-314.
Namkhai Norbu and Adriano Clemente, 1999: pp. 158-61.

Rdo la gser zhun: Pure Golden Ore
TB vol. Ka ff. 96.4-98.6; *Kun byed rgyal po* ch. 26.
TB vol. Ka ff. 450.3-453.3; *Mdo bcu*, in the eighth sutra.

Namkhai Norbu and Adriano Clemente, 1999: pp. 163-65.
Mi nub pa'i rgyal mtshan: Nam mkha' che
The Eternal Victory Banner: The Vast Space of Vajrasattva
TB vol. Ka ff. 105.2-113.1; *Kun byed rgyal po* ch. 30.
TB vol. Ka ff. 352-499 ; in the ten sutras of the *Mdo bcu*.
BGB vol. Nga 383-395.
Adriano Clemente, 1999.
Namkhai Norbu and Adriano Clemente, 1999: pp. 168-73.

Appendix II
Mind Series Jargon

NB. The following abbreviations are employed as indices in the subsequent analysis: CS = *Cuckoo's Song*; RC = *Radical Creativity*; GG = *Great Garuda*; PGO = *Pure Golden Ore*; and VB = *Victory Banner*. The 'c' denotes citation from the respective commentary.

The vocabulary of the transmissions helps to confirm these Mind Series texts as the earliest Dzogchen scriptures. Dzogchen terminology was still evidently in an incipient phase and had not developed into the jargon of later exegesis. It was as if Vairotsana was employing a common vocabulary to translate his experience, very much as we struggle to translate the Tibetan into English. The language of the *Mdo bcu* on the other hand is written in highly developed Dzogchen jargon and argues for a much later date of composition by an author other than Vairotsana. In the transmissions, for example, the words 'reality' (*chos nyid*) and surprisingly, 'gnosis' (*rig pa*) rarely appear, and likewise 'reality-field' (dharmadhatu) and 'pure being' (dharmakaya). The word 'matrix' or 'expanse' (*klong*), a vital notion in elaborated Dzogchen, does not appear in the transmissions and only once in the commentary. The term 'ground of being' (*kun gzhi*) does not appear (although see PGO2). The phrase 'nondual perception' (*gzung 'dzin med pa*) does not appear in the transmissions, although frequently in the *Mdo bcu* commentary. The term 'seminal nucleus' (*thig le chen po*) appears once in the transmissions (PGO10), although the notion of the 'one indivisible particle' (*rdul phran gcig*) (GG3) could present the germ of that concept. As to be expected the term 'emptiness' (*stong pa nyid*) does not appear in the transmissions (but see GG), although the commentary uses it occasionally.

Further, the transmissions do not mention the three dimensions of being (*trikaya*) and the commentary stresses the unity of the three as the one dharmakaya. Nor are the four yogas or the nine approaches mentioned, although one of the main themes of the *Mdo bcu* is the assimilation of the gradual approaches into radical Dzogchen. The commentary to *Victory Banner* verses 4, 5 and 6 applies the natural modality of the great perfection to mahayoga, anuyoga and outer yogatantra (sattva-yoga), where each is shown as complete and perfect. This is in apposition to the commentary to verses 42, 27, 36 and 17 upon the reality of anuyoga, mahayoga, tantra-yoga and atiyoga respectively, where anuyoga is described as a 'subtle technique', while mahayoga and tantra-yoga are considered faulted. The absence of these and other enumerations and frames of analysis in the transmissions argues a very early date and very pure antecedents for the Mind Series transmissions of radical Dzogchen.

Pure mind (bodhichitta, byang chub sems)
There is a strong case for assimilating the word *bodhichitta*, by which we understand the buddha's compassionate mind, into the English language, since we possess no precise equivalent. 'Enlightened' or 'awakened mind' is the phase most commonly employed in the vajrayana. But in the vajrayana enlightened mind is the prerogative of buddha only, whereas in Dzogchen it is the very stuff of all-embracing reality. Bodhichitta is reality itself—'pure mind and reality are one in the dharmadhatu' (RCc 1-2), as mind and inner space are one (GG1c). The nondual imperative of Dzogchen requires a more neutral, less affective, equivalent for bodhichitta and for that reason we have chosen 'pure mind', the pure mind that supersedes or transcends the rational mind without any sense of moral quality. Pure mind is also the sole recourse of beings trapped on a causal path because it is the one cause and the sole effect (GG19c). Pure mind, however, is also identified as loving kindness (VB1) and selfless compassion (GG14c). Since the term defines the Mind Series of Dzogchen precepts, its meaning is paramount and justifies its dominant incidence in the texts.

Pure essence of mind (byang chub snying po, bodhigarbha)
As the one cause, pure mind is the pure essence of mind, the source of all things (VB33c). 'Essence' is here a rendering of *snying po* which could also be translated as 'womb' or 'matrix'. However, 'essence' is to be understood as emptiness, never as even the most subtle concrete quintessence. Since pure mind is free of any substantial *ens* or self, the connotation of substance is always inappropriate. The physical image of the word 'womb' makes it inappropriate as an equivalent of *snying po* in the Dzogchen context because it implies a separation of the container and the contents. The pure essence of mind is *bodhichitta* as the sole cause, not to be separated from bodhichitta as the sole effect. The essence and the manifestation are one. The seed and the product are one. Pure essence of mind and pure mind are one.

Particularly in *Great Garuda* and *Pure Golden Ore*, 'pure essence of mind' replaces 'pure mind'. 'Pure essence of mind' is preferable because it denotes potentiality rather than actuality. Nothing ever comes into existence or ceases to be and remains therefore in a state of potential, as in a womb, which is the nature of pure mind, and is described as 'the great nucleus' (*thig le chen po*) and 'the six nuclei' (PGO11, PGO13). In *Great Garuda* the emergent nature of the pure essence of mind is pure being, 'individuated' emptiness (GG2). This essence is our all-inclusive identity and that is the wish-fulfilling gem (GG14c). It is all-encompassing creativity ('radical creativity') (GG22). In the pure essence of mind the ultimate samadhi arises as pristine awareness in the field of reality (GG23).

In *Pure Golden Ore* the pure essence of mind is identified with Manjushri Kumara, the all-inclusive buddha-body deity of the eight mahayoga buddhas, who is the fount of all phenomena and thus all experience. All such experience is spontaneously released in the pure essence of mind modality. Thus the essence of pure mind is 'the mother of the sugatas' (*sugatagarbha*). In the pure essence of mind, pure mind and the proclivities of mind are one—there is no separation. The nature of the pure essence of mind is self-sprung awareness, unchanging and imperturbable. It is inconceivable, always present like space, transcending ideas and speech.

In *Victory Banner* the pure essence of mind is the place of all suffering, where forever comprehended, never becoming anything more or less than pure mind, it manifests as pure being and pristine awareness (VB15c). All dualities are congruent in the pure essence of mind: therein buddha's pure pleasure and the happiness and misery of ordinary beings are one (VB10c). The reality of pleasure and pain, happiness and sadness and the five passions is identical in the pure essence of mind. Man and woman are identical in the pure essence of mind (VB33). The field of reality in the pure essence of mind remains unmoved by mentation (VB11). Desire, anger and bewilderment arise in the modality of the pure essence of mind (VB16c). 'The pure essence of mind is the universal source and pure and simple reality', at once indeterminate reality itself and the source of reality (VB22).

Reality (chos nyid, dharmata)
The Dzogchen reality of pure mind is nondual reality and that is all that should be said about it. Insofar as the view and meditation of atiyoga is a constant recognition of deconstructed mind and experience, it provides

that reality. Etymologically both the Sanskrit and the Tibetan words mean 'experience (*dharma*) in itself'. The word appears only seven times in the transmissions—although surely reality is their nature and their purpose: it is not exclusive to any particular experience or phenomena (RC5); it is free and open and all-inclusive (GG18); unsought, it is known in nonmeditation (VB7); it cannot be transmitted through time (VB8); it is adorned by sensual pleasure in the dharmadhatu (VB16); it is pure and simple and cannot be elaborated (VB22); and it is noncontingent (VB41).

Reality is inexpressible and the adjectives used to describe it in the *Mdo bcu* all point to that ineffability through negation. It is nondual (CSc), superseding time (VB48c) and space (VB31c), pleasure and pain (VB15c) and the five passions (VB15c); it is not created (CSc and VB6c), it is nondiscursive (GG1c); it cannot be located (GG3c) and it cannot be discovered ; it cannot be objectified (GG12c); it is insubstantial (GG15c); it is unelaborated and indeterminable (VB12c); it is immovable (VB3c) and unchangeable (VB41-43); it is signless (VB21c); and it cannot be accomplished or attested (VB55c).

On the other hand, reality is defined positively as Vajrasattva, pure mind (RC2c and VB16c), as the here-and-now ('suchness') (CSc), as pristine awareness (GG3c), as equality (GG3c), as our dharmakaya identity (VB3c), as one totality (VB22c); its nature is spontaneous pure pleasure (VB26c); it is a display of bliss (GG5c); it is the Dzogchen modality itself (VB24c); it is identical to loving kindness and compassion (VB2c). It is a timeless unchanging moment (VB41-43).

The field of reality (chos dbyings, dharmadhatu)
The first distinction to be made in the temporal development of consciousness in childhood is between inside and outside, subject and object. The tendency to concretization of self and other dominates our ordinary perception, but the reality is a unified field of experience that viewed holistically is called the dharmadhatu. The first three verses of *Radical Creativity* describe it as Samantabhadra's emanation, which is our own field of experience. It is a unitary field superseding all outer and inner distinctions and time itself (VB26). It is a field of absolute identity and equality. It is perfect in itself, unalterable and immovable. It is a dynamic field of experience free of any directed activity and thus it can be described as a 'freeform field' (RC3c). In the first two verses of *Great Garuda*, Samantabhadra's emanation as the dharmadhatu is shown

'individuated' as the mind of the Dzogchen yogin and therefore as the Dzogchen modality in which a field, as pure mind, cannot be anywhere located, a non-field in perceptual nonduality, nondiscursive and non-analytical. Although it is 'individuated', the dharmadhatu is still unlimited, uncircumscribed, without center or circumference (GG5).

If Samantabhadra is the nondual wholeness of being and knowing, Vajrasattva is the vast spaciousness of the field of reality within pure being, or 'individuated emptiness' (VB1). The field of reality is thus the space in which all and everything agglomerates and is reflexively released as Vajrasattva in a constant unimpeded process. 'Dharmadhatu' may be rendered simply as spaciousness or as 'existential space'.

In the anuyoga view the reality-field is posited as the complement of gnosis (*rig pa*) in a union of the gender principles of skillful means and insight. Thus the Dzogchen unity of the single Samantabhadra is provisionally split to show Samantabhadra as gnosis in union with Samantabhadri as reality itself (VB5).

The five passions arise in pure mind and the five sensual pleasures are described as 'ornaments' of the field of reality. As such they partake of the nature of reality and therefore can have no appearance, no form, shape or color (VB16). In the same way, the universe as an offering of sensual pleasure is described in terms of an 'adornment' of the field of reality, so the offering is an offering of the dharmadhatu as emptiness (VB49).

Pure being (dharmakaya, chos sku)
If the dharmadhatu refers to the holistic experiential field, the dharmakaya refers to the ontic dimension of the totality, to pure being. The word 'being' in English, within its abstract universal meaning, has a personalized sense that allows the notion of buddha in human form. This limitation, however, is belied by its definition as 'unthought sameness' (VB18), which is a close synonym of 'emptiness' a term rarely used in Dzogchen exegesis. 'Pure mind reality is like space, and mind without thought is pure being' (VB18c). Within pure being pure mind reality lacks any concrete name or form whatsoever—it is utterly insubstantial—so there is nothing to grasp and hold on to. Within the unoriginated dharmakaya of Samantabhadra the magical illusion of creation is apparent and all of creation is Samantabhadra's display.

'Within pure being magical illusion arises composed of the five aggregates which as secondary emanations of the eight consciousnesses comprise the complete sphere of activity of the three-fold mundane finite world which takes the form of the five passions' five sensory pleasures' (VB26c). In this sense pure being is all-inclusive. But since pure mind never becomes any thing, never becomes any shape, size or color, and, therefore, insofar as it never moves out of its own nature, it is immovable and unchangeable (VB32c), and known as pure being, present as the stance (mudra) of pure being, and as a seal of pure being, it is free of perceptual duality. The self-sprung awareness of pure being remains constant in an imperturbable samadhi. So pure being is pristine awareness.

In *Great Garuda* (verses 1-3) a distinction is made between the notional dharmakaya which is the object of goal-oriented meditation and pure being that is pristine awareness. The notional dharmakaya as a concept refers to nothing at all and, therefore, simultaneous with its conception self-sprung awareness arises. The same may be said for any concept whatsoever, so all thought is pure being.

Pristine awareness (ye shes, jnana)
This basic awareness is forever fresh, never becoming tired, bored or jaded. There is an element of the ingenuousness of the simpleton in it since it cannot be elaborated into a complex proposition. Since it is nondual perception, nothing can transcend it and it cannot be objectified; it can therefore be rendered as 'ultimate awareness'. Since it exists as original reality, it can be rendered as 'primordial awareness'. It has no cause or condition and arises spontaneously by and of itself and it is thus 'self-sprung awareness'. Direct perception and nondual cognition are pristine awareness in the reality-field that is all pure mind; it is spontaneous, instantaneous cognition. It cannot be discovered by seeking (VB20c) and it is immune to analysis (VB25c). It arises in an unimpeded samadhi (VB1c), imperturbable (VB32). Nothing can induce it or develop it. The process of release is inherent within it (VB3). It's nature is natural pure pleasure (VB26c). Gnosis is a function of pristine awareness (VB42).

Thought itself is pristine awareness because the dharmakaya as a concept is naturally indeterminate and pure (GG1). Thought in itself is thought-free and pristine awareness is 'a ubiquitous, natural presence' (GG1). It has no location, no specifics, and it is noncomposite (GG3c). It transcends all thought and expression, absorbing all specific meaning in one single sovereign equality. The field of reality is spontaneously and constantly suffused by pristine awareness. Pristine awareness is a wish-fulfilling jewel (GG12). Pristine awareness is the eye of direct insight, the eye of omniscience, that sees the nature of the field of reality (PGO6).

Although it cannot be located, it can be recognized in the natural union of means and insight (anuyoga) (VB5). Desire, anger and bewilderment arise as pristine awareness (VB16). Pristine awareness arises particularly in the state of bewilderment as Samantabhadra's miraculous display (VB44). It spontaneously arises in thought (VB12), in the spaciousness of mental constructs (anuyoga) (VB17). In the perspective of sattva-yoga, the buddha-deity of pristine awareness identifies with the yogi. In ubhaya-yoga vision, pristine awareness is radiated from the nature of mind as Vajrasattva who is inseparable from the five colors and the five elements (VB47c). In the offering ritual the offering of the sensual pleasures, the individuated mind that is making the offering and pristine awareness are one (VB49c).

Bewilderment (*gti mug*), or a state of stupidity, is clouded pristine awareness that possesses the same undiscriminating facility as pristine awareness itself and therefore pristine awareness arises easily within it, or rather it is timelessly inherent in it and spontaneously emerges therein (PGO5). The scriptures themselves and momentary visions appear in pulsating nescience (GG19).

Pure being and pristine awareness (sku dang ye shes)
Pure mind has no structure, yet it is described didactically in terms of being (*sku*) and awareness (*ye shes*), a putative dualism of its ontic and epistemic aspects (VB6c). 'Pure being' refers to the structure of reality, or since this structure has no concrete reality and no temporal or spatial limitations perhaps 'anti-structure' is more meaningful. It could be described as the uni-dimensional reality of pure mind, since it is not elaborated in time or space, yet it appears as variegated multiplicity. This structure may be differentiated as the three modes of pure being—dharmakaya, sambhogakaya and nirmanakaya—but such a distinction is mentioned only once in the five transmissions and that in the commentary. Pristine awareness is the all-inclusive pure cognition of all buddha. So pure being is pure mind and pristine awareness its innate

propensity for cognition. As a skillful means, realization of the unity of the ontic (*sku*) and epistemic (*ye shes*) voids substantiality in the sensory fields by facilitating the union of subject and object. They are united as a union of 'the immovable' and 'the imperturbable' (VB32c).

The all-inclusive magical illusion of pure mind is actualized by an involuntary realization of its unitary nature of 'suchness'. Then it can be described as indivisible 'pure being' in its ontic reality and 'pristine awareness' in its epistemic aspect (VB6c). Likewise, in realization of the wheel of life as the modality of pure mind, the phantasmagoric display is a union of pure being and the five aspects of pristine awareness (VB9c). Again, in so far as the field of buddha-experience is devoid of perceptual duality—any structure based on consciousness, sense organ and sensory object, the fictions of dualistic analysis—buddha-experience in pure being is described in terms of pure being and pristine awareness (VB20c).

Nature of mind (sems nyid)
The seminal phrase the 'nature of mind' does not appear in the transmissions. Pure mind and the pure essence of mind are the nature of mind and subsume all its meanings.

Path, process, modality (lam)
If a path implies a distinct starting point, a temporal progression and a destination Dzogchen Ati has no path—or it is better designated a pathless path, the path always under our feet that has no extension. And yet within a timeless moment of pure mind there is an unfoldment and a release. For this reason 'path' has sometimes been rendered as 'process'. To emphasize the synchronistic function of 'arising', 'abiding' and 'releasing', 'modality' has sometimes been preferred to 'path' or 'process'.

Equality, sameness (mnyam pa, mnyam nyid)
'Equality' describes the nature of Samantabhadra himself who is the Lord of Equality, and 'sovereign equality' is the nature of pure mind, the pure mind matrix, and therefore of all things whatsoever. This 'equality' is synonymous with 'identity' in the sense that the nature of mind is identical in every moment of the here-and-now. Equality is an attribute of the ocean and also of the sky. Equality, however, is a state of being, a state of 'evenness' or 'equanimity', in which there is no radiation or absorption. In its imperturbability, it is the antidote to desire and

attachment. At the same time it is present in the active sphere of Samantabhadra and as such is both the intrinsic identity of multiplicity and multiplicity itself, in the same way that reality is both pure mind matrix and pure mind manifest. In this way equality is virtually synonymous with emptiness (*stong pa nyid*) though it has a stronger, positive flavor. It is the nature of gnosis (*rig pa*). It is the unthought dharmakaya. It is reality (*chos nyid*) itself.

'Equality', in Tibetan, as it does in English, carries the sense of 'on the ground' and thus is 'free of all complacency and arrogance'. 'Equality', besides taking the sting out of desire and attachment, is the antidote to guilt and remorse. Indeed, the state of equality can be fully recognized through sexual indulgence and anti-social activity. It is this fundamental quality of pure mind that brings the sage and the sinner onto a level playing field.

Nonaction, freeform (bya med, bya bral)
'Nonaction' may imply the unmoving nature of the reality-field (GG1), the dharmadhatu itself (GG1c), but it is, simultaneously, the play of sameness or emptiness in multiplicity and for that reason it has been rendered 'freeform', like the sky, herein. Nonaction is 'non-directed action' or 'spontaneous, freeform action' (RC3); it is spontaneity itself. It is the yogi's activity that is an integral part of the dynamic, miraculous display of Samantabhadra (GG24). There is no self-directed motivation, and indeed there is no motivation whatsoever. There is no effort involved, no goal-oriented striving, no seeking for the sake of finding (VB55c). There is no connotation of 'hard work' or 'onerous duty'. It may imply renunciation of all mundane involvement, but not necessarily so. It may imply the abandonment of all spiritual materialism, including meditation, devotional exercises and ritual, but again not necessarily so (VB21). This definition is inclining towards 'nonaction' as an attitude to the dynamic of 'body', 'speech' and 'mind' (VB53). With this attitude the spectacular display of appearances, including the yogin, is a constant, but nothing is ever done. At the same time everything is released (VB3).

The Five Early Translations belong to those chapters of the *Kun byed rgyal po* which treat perfected nonaction. But the word appears only rarely therein and rarely in the *Mdo bcu* commentary. Its significance, however, is seminal in Dzogchen exegesis.

Appendices

Gnosis (rig pa)
Rigpa is best defined as nondual awareness of our every moment of experience. As the verb 'to know' in dualistic verbal structures it was elevated in Dzogchen jargon to denote the realization of natural perfection. Since we have no equivalent of this notion in the English language we have used the word 'gnosis' herein, a word that should be taken to imply full awareness of the nondual holistic natural state of being. The word appears only once in the Transmissions where it is used to describe Samantabhadra's pure-pleasure awareness (VB42) and then infrequently in the commentary to the *Victory Banner*, which indicates a late movement to the center of Dzogchen exegesis. Here gnosis is the transcendental realization that subsumes all conceptual meditation (VB13c). It cannot be cultivated, and intrinsic to unstructured reality it is free of dualistic perception; discursive thought arising therein is pristine awareness itself (VB12c). Here gnosis would be represented iconographically as the single naked blue buddha Samantabhadra. But this gnostic totality is also described as a timeless union of gnosis and the dharmadhatu, in which gnosis is the skillful means and reality-field the insight function (VB5c). Likewise, whereas the reality-field is represented by the vowels of articulated expression, so gnosis is represented by the consonants (VB18c). The union of vowels and consonants is the display of Samantabhadra that never crystalizes. This display of spontaneity is a dance of gnosis (VB52c). In the radical Dzogchen of the transmissions, it is hard to avoid the conclusion that rigpa is knowledge of the common light of day.

Union (sbyor ba)
The notion of 'union', sexual or metaphysical, belongs in the tantric domain. Yet sexual union as the spontaneous play of Samantabhadra's emanation is buddha-activity (RC4) and his display itself may be conceived as the union of vowels and consonants (VB18-19). In commentary on the *Victory Banner*, the union of skillful means and insight is treated under the rubric of anuyoga (VB5). Where in tantra-yoga the notion of union would be employed there is circumlocution to indicate a timeless immanent interfusion (VB34), which may appear as a flash of spontaneous cognition or 'nonunion' (VB52). In the deconstruction of the tantric ganachakra rite, union is a timeless, endless dance (VB52c).

Appendices

Realization (rtogs pa)
The word *rtogs pa*, often translated as 'realization' or 'intuitive understanding', is linguistically rooted in the verb *rtog pa* 'to think'. Mental structure and thought as functions of the rational, intellectual mind are coincident with realization of the nature of mind as empty and radiant (RCc). The modality of natural perfection is inherent in every thought-form. In later Dzogchen exegesis, thought, or the stream of discursive mentation (*rnam rtog*), is conceived of more as a glitch in the pure mind modality, rather than as a basis for realization. Insofar as we know reality as nothing other than mental constructs we are never free of 'realization'. In the Transmissions, and particularly in VBc, thought, like passion, is inseparable from pure mind itself and therefore never to be avoided or suppressed. The seemingly indiscriminate use of *rtog pa* and *rtogs pa* in the texts may be an error of grammar or calligraphy but their proximate identity is thereby indicated.

Field, object (yul)
In the delusive dualistic analysis of perception, objects of the senses, the objective field, is grasped by consciousness, 'the knower'. In nondual perception there is no object to grasp and the sensory fields are the field of reality, the dharmadhatu.

Buddha (sang rgyas pa)
In the Dzogchen view there are no separate entities called 'buddhas'. Rather, there is universal buddhahood, which is synonymous with enlightenment.

Body, speech and mind (sku gsung thugs)
The three dimensions of 'body', 'speech' and 'mind' are one in pure mind and one in pure being. The elaboration of the fundamental unity into three aspects provides a skillful means of illuminating the delusive miasmas of the six kinds of being in three dimensions. Human 'body', 'speech' and 'mind' refers to the dimensions of structured emanational being, energy flows and patterns, and consciousness, respectively. Buddha 'body', 'speech' and 'mind' refers to the natural equality of those dimensions in pure mind. Buddha 'body', 'speech' and 'mind' are like the eyes of pure mind that recognize the variety of beings, the passions, the suffering and the sensual pleasures on the wheel of life, as pure mind. More specifically, buddha 'body', 'speech' and 'mind' are the purity of the three poisons in pure mind, 'buddha-body' recognizing the tendency

to attraction and desire and its manifestations, 'buddha-speech' recognizing the tendency to aversion and anger, and 'buddha-mind' recognizing all forms of bewilderment and ignorance. In conceptual meditation the centers of 'body', 'speech' and 'mind' are located in the head, throat and heart respectively.

Selected Bibliography

Clemente, A. *The Total Space of Vajrasattva*. Shang Shung Edizioni, 1999.

Dowman, Keith. *The Flight of the Garuda*. Revised edition. Boston, Wisdom, 2003.

Dudjom Lingpa. *Buddhahood Without Meditation*. Trans. Richard Barron. Padma Publishing, 1994.

Dudjom Rinpoche *The Nyingma School of Tibetan Buddhism: Its Fundamentals and History*. 2 vols. Trans. Gyurme Dorje and Matthew Kapstein. Boston, Wisdom, 1991.

Germano, D. "Poetic Thought, the Intelligent Universe, and the Mystery of Self: The Tantric Synthesis of Dzogchen in Fourteenth Century Tibet", unpublished doctoral dissertation, 1992.

-----."The Funerary Transformation of the Great Perfection", *Journal of the International Association of Tibetan Studies*, no.1 (October 2005): pp. 1-54.

Guenther, H. *Matrix of Mystery*. Boulder, Shambhala, 1984.

Low, James. *Simply Being*. Vajra Press, London, 1998,

Longchenpa. *Old Man Basking in the Sun: Longchenpa's Treasury of Natural Perfection*. Trans. Keith Dowman. Kathmandu, Vajra Books, 2006.

Longchenpa. *You Are the Eyes of the World*. Trans. Kennard Lipman and Merrill Peterson with Namkhai Norbu. Lotsava, 1987.

Namkhai Norbu and Shane, John. *The Crystal and the Way of Light*. London, RKP, 1986.

Namkhai Norbu and Lipman, Kennard. *Primordial Experience*. Boston, Shambhala, 1987.

Namkhai Norbu and Clemente, Adriano. *Dzogchen: the Self-Perfected State*. London, Arkana, 1989.

-----. *The Supreme Source: The Fundamental Tantra of the Dzogchen Semde*. Ithica, Snow Lion, 1999.

Nyoshul Khenpo *Natural Great Perfection*. Trans. Surya Das. Ithaca, Snow Lion, 1995.

Reynolds, J. *Golden Letters*. Ithica, Snow Lion, 1996.

Samten Karmay. *The Great Perfection*. Leyden, Brill, 1988.

Selected Bibliography

Tulku Thondup. *Buddha Mind: An Anthology of Longchen Rabjampa's Writing on Dzogpa Chenpo.* Ithica, Snow Lion, 1989.
Yudra Nyingpo. *The Great Image: The Life Story of Vairochana the Translator.* Trans. Ani Jinba Palmo. Ithaca, Snow Lion, 2004.